DON'T DRINK THE WATER!

A STORY ABOUT GOD'S SAVING GRACE

BY

SANDY LUDWIG

Don't Drink the Water!
Published: September 2019
Printed in the United States of America
ISBN: 9781689385985

This book was published with the assistance of Self-Publishing Relief, a division of Writer's Relief.

ACKNOWLEDGMENTS

I acknowledge and thank Suzan Eubank, my editor and friend, for reading the first drafts of my book, for making creative suggestions and for gently (read laughingly) correcting my grammar and typo mistakes. Suzan kept me focused with lots of encouragement and positive support.

Next I thank my two college classmates, Loretta (Bush) Wittkopp and Carol (Lilliard) Leamon, for showing me the flyer about teaching fellowships in Colombia and encouraging me to apply for one. They were my chief supporters and cheerleaders who helped me get to what I hoped would be a great adventure.

Sue Harmer is next for offering her computer expertise; Don Howland for turning me onto self-publishing; and Janet Bek, Betty Mitchell and Mike McHale for helping me with computer problems.

Most of all I thank my wonderful, supportive, long-suffering husband who put up with all the time it took me to write the book and then to edit, edit, edit it! He thought it would never end! However, through it all, he was very encouraging and proud of me, and happily informed our friends and neighbors about the book.

Finally, I wish to thank my children, Kris, Janis and Randy, who encouraged me to follow through on my dream to publish my book.

Sandy Ludwig
July 2019

DISCLAIMERS AND DEDICATION

All names in the book are fictitious except for my family, my two college friends and myself.

All Scripture quotations are taken from the <u>New Revised Standard Version</u> of the Bible, printed in 1989 by the Oxford University Press, Inc. The original Revised Standard Version of the Bible was presented as a gift to every student arriving at Elmhurst College in the Fall of 1962. This was the newest Bible available at the time and I proudly accepted my copy as a returning Senior, and took it with me to Colombia in June 1963. However, the Biblical quotes in the book have been taken from the new revised standard version because the English is more up to date.

This book is dedicated to my precious Nana for living her faith so fully and for instilling that faith in me.

Elva Melegari

1890-1993

TABLE OF CONTENTS

INTO THE WILDERNESS

It all began when my two closest friends, Lori and Carol, came barging into my dorm room at Elmhurst College to present me with a wonderful opportunity. I was sitting at my desk studying for final exams, my mind at that moment on a list of Spanish verbs I was trying to memorize for the exam just a few days away.

Their excited chatter broke my concentration and I was about to ask them if they would please quiet down, when they surrounded me at my desk, hovering over me with excitement written all over their faces. Both were grinning from ear to ear, just bursting to tell me something. I grinned back at them, tentatively, not sure what was going on. Carol was a pretty brunette with an engaging smile and a beautiful singing voice. Lori, my suitemate, was petite, with big glasses, eyes full of mischief, and curly hair.

Before I tell you what they were so excited about, let me introduce myself. My name is Sandra – preferably Sandy – Cone, and if you're wondering if I was ever teased much about my last name, the answer is yes! I was teased, a lot. I was constantly asked what flavor ice cream I was and my answer was always the same: *vanilla*. The second question was a response to my answer, "How come you're always *vanilla* and not chocolate or strawberry?" All I could tell them was that I liked it the best. But, if you ask my brother, I told everyone, he'll tell you he's a chocolate Cone. But I digress.

I have to describe myself as a shorty, standing 5'1" (well, to be honest, 5'1/2") and a little chubby, weighing about 120 lbs. I have short dark curly hair, brown eyes and wear glasses. I guess I'm more brainy than good-looking, more introverted than extroverted and a dreamer more than a realist.

After nineteen years of education (I started at age three), I pined for something different, like. . .an *adventure!* It could last for a summer, a year, or five years. I dearly needed a break! I longed to go to some exotic land to meet people from a different culture, and to use my Spanish which I've been studying for seven years. Call it a flight from reality, if you want. I just wanted to do something totally different from studying and working my way through school.

Now, interrupted in my studies by Lori and Carol standing over me at my desk, waving a flyer in my face, I looked up at their grinning faces and wondered what was going on.

"Sandy, look what we found!" Lori announced excitedly.

"What?"

"Look at it!" She put the flyer in my hand and waited impatiently for me to read it. I scanned it as quickly as I could.

"A teaching fellowship in Colombia, South America?" I questioned.

"Yes!" said Lori. "We thought it might be the kind of adventure you were looking for and you'd get to use your Spanish. Just read it, you'll see." It immediately became clear to me: they had heard me talking about going on a grand adventure after we graduated from Elmhurst at the end of this month, and had decided to help me out.

So I read the flyer more thoroughly. It told me about teaching positions in seven different cities in Colombia, South America, at American-sponsored language schools. I recognized the name Bogotá, the capital of Colombia, but knew little else about the country. I was vaguely aware that Colombia produced illegal drugs and communism was on the rise there. Did an American 'government-sponsored' language school mean I was going to be thrust into the middle of drug wars and communism? Hmmm.

"What do you think?" asked Carol. "Doesn't it look like fun?" I shook the negative thoughts out of my head so I could answer that it certainly sounded interesting. But before I even got the first word out, Carol pointed out that it was a year-long assignment, no experience required (except knowing Spanish, of course). It would begin in early June of this year (yikes, less than a month away!) and all travel expenses were covered! That all sounded absolutely terrific!

I read the flyer again more slowly, with Lori and Carol pointing out things that seemed important. For instance, the purpose of the schools was to combat the rise of communism in Colombia by teaching English and taking films out to the *barrios*, which were outlying neighborhoods and tiny communities surrounding the big cities. There was always one film that promoted democratic ideals, and other films showing farmers new ways to produce healthy crops, along with cartoons for the kids and regular Hollywood movies. My job, should I get it, would be to teach English at one of the schools. That sounded safe enough.

As soon as I looked up, Lori suggested that I apply for one of the positions down there today, right now!

"But the flyer says the application needed to be in by *last* week," I protested.

"So?" responded Carol. "Give it a try anyway. What have you got to lose?" Indeed, what did I have to lose? Nothing. Even if it was too late to get selected, I would have at least made a stab at doing something different. Of course, if I got one of the teaching positions, I wasn't getting too far away from school stuff, was I? Ah, I thought, but teaching others is very different than being taught, right? It would be a complete reversal of roles. I could live with that.

So that very day I filled out an application and mailed it off. I didn't believe I had a chance, mainly because it was way past the deadline, but it had been hard to say no to two of my closest friends. While I waited for a reply, I secretly grew more and more excited about the possibility of going. I found myself praying for a reply that said, 'Yes! You're hired!' It would be fun and challenging to teach non-English speaking people and to use the Spanish I'd been studying for so long. After Lori and Carol left, I sat there by myself a while contemplating this opportunity. It started me thinking about how I got to this point in my life.

It all began with Nana, my grandmother, with whom I lived most of my growing-up years. God guided me into a strong personal faith with Nana as my role model. Though I grew to understand that my faith was ultimately a gift from God, it was through Nana that I learned how a Christian was supposed to live.

Nana – and therefore I – were devoted to our church, which we attended faithfully. She also went out of her way to feed and visit sick and homebound church members and neighbors. Not having a car, they had to be people within walking distance. Nana's faith and loving-kindness rubbed off on me, as God had planned. Every night, it was our custom to read the Bible together, then get down on our knees and pray the Lord's Prayer together, then, silently, our personal prayers. Because

Nana lived her faith so fully, she encouraged me to. When I was in high school, I attended the Youth Fellowship group, taught second grade Sunday school and sang in the choir.

I chose to come here to Elmhurst College because it was affiliated with my denomination, the United Church of Christ. I took all the religion courses I could to learn as much as possible about the Bible and what God wanted me to know and do. I had what I called a "Sunday school faith" when I arrived, that is, a child-like faith, but I yearned for an adult faith that would help me deal with the grownup realities of life. Yes, I loved the dramatic, memorable stories of the Old Testament, but Jesus' parables, stories and healings in the New Testament spoke especially to my heart. Through Jesus, I came to believe that God loves all His children, that He created everyone, regardless of our color, the life choices we make, or the way we worship God. Jesus the Christ, the Son of God, spoke to my heart and I felt God calling me to become a minister to continue His message of love, acceptance and compassion to other people.

After graduating from Elmhurst at the end of the month, my plan – after my longed-for fantasy adventure, of course – was to go to Lancaster Seminary in Pennsylvania, where I hoped to pull my faith together into a comprehensive whole and prepare for ordained ministry. This would prepare me for my life's work. We have sixty-six God-inspired books in the Bible to teach us about God's love, judgment and mercy. I wanted to take the faith of thousands of generations of Christians, make it my own, and share it with others.

After Lancaster, I hoped to become a missionary to Honduras.

.   .   .

That's the threshold where I stood on May 13, 1963. Graduation loomed, and then freedom to fly into fantasyland and live an adventure before settling back down to earth and the rest of my life.

As I waited for a reply from the government agency sponsoring the schools, I developed some misgivings about going to Colombia, should I be accepted. I dropped slowly to my knees at my bed and prayed. *Dear Lord, is it Your will that I go to Colombia, if the opportunity becomes available, or is it just* my *will? If I do go, will I have a chance to share my faith and help people in need? And what will my role be in a government-sponsored language school in a country where communists are stirring up trouble and drug wars abound? Give me clarity and understanding of what my role as a Christian should be there. Please enlighten me, Father, and help me make the right decision about going.*

No soothing peacefulness settled over me to assure me that God had heard my prayer and would bless my year abroad. This was one of the few times in my life that I didn't feel God's response. I had never made a decision as momentous as this before, without getting God's yes first. What should I do? Should I wait and see if I got accepted? If I did get accepted, should I consider that God's yes? If not, His no? I didn't feel altogether comfortable with that decision, but that's where I left it for the time being.

I checked my mailbox every day for a reply from the government agency offering the teaching fellowship. Finally, it came. I left the envelope sealed and ran back to the dorm, all excited. Lori and Carol sat with me on my bed while I hastily opened the envelope. My heart was pounding and I held my breath as I unfolded the letter and read it. I was hopeful yet reminded myself repeatedly how late my application had been.

Lori asked excited, "What does it say?"

I met hers and Carol's eager eyes and broke into a slow but very wide smile. "I've been accepted!" I told them unbelievingly. "I've been accepted!! I can't believe it!"

"Where will you be going?" asked Carol. "Which city?"

"The name of the city is Cartagena. I've never heard of it, but then I never heard of the other cities listed on the flyer, either, except Bogotá."

"When do you leave?" asked Lori.

"On June 2nd! That barely a week after graduation!"

Both friends grabbed me and hugged me, and we danced around the room. I thanked them for bringing the flyer to me and for encouraging me to apply. They congratulated me on getting the position.

I also thanked God, feeling sure that this meant He was giving me His yes to go to Colombia. After Lori and Carol left, I got on my knees and prayed. *Lord, please bless this trip. Please protect and guide me while I'm there. Let me find ways to serve You and honor Your Name through all that I do there.*

I felt it then, a sense of God's presence surrounding me and His peace filling me with His love and His acceptance.

Let the fun begin!

Ah, but before all the fun could begin, I had many things to do. I had to get a passport and shots for illnesses like typhoid fever and malaria and some other tropical diseases I'd never heard of. And, of course, I had to fill out lots of paperwork on myself, my health, my education, my Spanish language proficiency, etc. I also had to notify Lancaster Seminary that I wouldn't be attending this coming fall after all and requested enrollment for the following year. They made the change.

To my amazement, I got everything done that I had to for my adventure in South America. In the midst of doing all that, I took my Spanish exam and passed with an A+! As soon as the exam was over, I raced back to my dorm room and started packing. Graduation was quickly approaching on May 28th and my family would be arriving soon for the occasion. I didn't graduate at the top of my class, but I had made the Dean's List. When the graduation ceremony was over, we students enthusiastically tossed our tasseled caps into the air and cheered. We'd made it!

Mom and Don, my parents, Nana, and Phil, my brother, had all come for the ceremony. They cheered and whooped as I got my diploma. Afterwards Don took pictures to memorialize it. I was the first in my family to graduate from college and they were proud of me. I shrugged out of my gown and we all linked arms and headed for my dorm to load up my stuff and head home.

For clarification, Don is Mom's second husband. They have been together for twelve years. Phil was raised by our paternal grandmother (also called Nana), since Mom and my father divorced when Phil and I were babies. My Nana raised me and I felt indebted to her for her willingness to take me in when she was fifty-plus years old. I was well aware of how much she had given up to raise me, and I was grateful to her for that as well as for sharing her faith with me and guiding me into a lifetime of commitment and service to the Lord. She even gave me her entire savings account of $500.00 so I could go to college!

It was time now to finish up the packing in my dorm room and start on the long drive home. When we were done packing up, Phil and Don carried my suitcases, satchel, and boxes of stuff down to the car, packed it all in, and off we set for Buffalo, a 550-mile trip. We stopped after a few hours and spent the night in a motel, then finished the trip the next day. Since Mom and Don were late risers, it was late Wednesday by the time we got home. We were all too tired to do much but wash up and get ready for bed.

Thursday dawned and I was too excited to stay in bed. I showered, unpacked my two suitcases and satchel, collecting the dirty laundry together in a pile, and then repacked the suitcases with the clothes and things that I would be taking to Cartagena. I decided my two suitcases and my trusty satchel would be enough. They were old but still serviceable.

Since I had received scant information about Cartagena, Colombia from the sponsoring government agency, Don pulled out one of the volumes from his set of Encyclopedia Britannica (which is the company he worked for as a traveling salesman) later that morning and we looked them up. Colombia was situated in the northwestern part of South America, I saw, and Cartagena was located in the northwestern tip of Colombia, right on the Caribbean Sea.

I noticed that Colombia was bordered by Venezuela and Brazil to the East, Ecuador and Peru to the south, and both the Caribbean Sea and the Pacific Ocean to the west. The Panama Canal joined Colombia at a point just south of Cartagena.

Being on the Caribbean like it was, Cartagena was a true port city. The pictures of it showed colorful painted homes and apartment buildings, delightful plazas, and lush foliage. The women wore bright clothes and the men were *serapes*, which were multi-colored shawl-like blankets worn over their shoulder. The city itself was known for its walls, which surrounded the city. The walls were constructed with massive stones piled high, built between the 1500's and the 1700's. I was surprised and amused to read that the walls were built to prevent pirates from entering and looting the city. How intriguing that sounded! There were seven miles of walls surrounding the city. I could hardly wait to get there and see it for myself!

By noon, I was as packed and ready as I could be. Everything was falling into place so nicely and easily – everything, that is, except the arrival of my passport! I waited on pins and needles for the mail to arrive that day and then again on Friday. By Saturday, I was in a nervous tizzy. I needed my passport to arrive today or I wouldn't be going anywhere tomorrow!

I retreated to my room, got on my knees and prayed fervently. *Please, Lord, You granted my prayer to go on this adventure. I felt like*

You were blessing it, that it was Your will. Is this your will, Father, that my passport not come in time, preventing me from making the trip after all? Please, Father, let the passport arrive today! I will be faithful to You the whole time I'm down in Cartagena. I will read my Bible and pray every day. I will reach out and help anyone who needs it. I will find a church to attend.

I continued kneeling, mulling over the words of my prayer. Jesus said, *"Ask, and it will be given you"* (Matthew 7:7), and so I had asked. But it dawned on me that I had bargained with God, too. Do this for me and I'll do something for You. I sighed, and after some minutes, I came to the same conclusion as I had before. If the passport arrived today, God was blessing this trip. If it didn't come, God's answer was clearly no. Either way, I told myself, I would be satisfied. If I were to go, wonderful. If not, I would find a job in a library for the summer and arrange to go to seminary in the fall, as originally planned.

Then I stood up, sighed deeply and joined my family downstairs. They, too, I saw, waited anxiously for the mail to arrive. Don played with his dog, Boy. Mom and Nana were reading books. I plopped down on the couch and waited impatiently for the mailman to arrive.

Which he finally did two hours later. I was hesitant to go out for the mail, afraid the passport wouldn't be there, but I reminded myself that I was going to accept the Lord's decision whichever it was.

"Well, Sandra," commented Nana (she never got used to calling me Sandy), "Go out and get the mail. Sitting there stewing over it isn't going to do you any good." Nana, with her head of white hair, old-styled glasses and sensible shoes, looked stern, but I knew it was only anxiety about the passport and the trip abroad.

Mom said, "Go already!" with a twinkle in her eye.

I returned from the mailbox with several letters, but only one held my interest. Gripping the official-looking envelope close to my chest, I handed the rest of the mail to Mom. I flopped onto the couch and ripped the envelope open. Everyone watched as I pulled out a perfect new passport with the United States emblem on the front of it and a picture of me inside! I crushed it to my chest. I was going! *Thank You, Father Almighty, thank you for Your yes!* I held it up for everyone to see and they broke into smiles of relief and happiness for me. I raced upstairs to place my passport in a protected pocket of my satchel.

.   .   .

My parents and precious Nana saw me off at the airport early in the evening of Sunday, June 2nd. I tried to act cool and professional but I was too excited and nervous to pull it off. Finally, it was time to kiss and hug everyone goodbye and board the plane. They waved, and I waved back, until we couldn't see each other anymore. Then I settled down in my seat and tried to relax on the way to New York City, where I would meet up with the six other people who had been selected for teaching fellowships in Colombia.

At the airport in New York, I saw four gals and two guys standing in a group, looking around for someone. I tentatively headed toward them and, when they saw me approaching them, they came toward me.

"Going to Colombia to teach?" asked one of the gals. I nodded. "Great! You're just in time. Join us." I did. Apparently we all had to fly to New York City to board this particular flight to Colombia. We took a few moments to introduce ourselves and chatted briefly. About a half hour later came the announcement for boarding the plane to Barranquilla, Colombia. As the door to the plane closed and the plane prepared for take-off, we settled into our seats, all thinking the same thought: next stop: *Colombia!!*

We tried to sit near each other on the plane, so we could talk about the cities we'd be going to. We each knew the name of our assigned city, so we took time to compare notes. The two others in my row said they were going to Cali and Barranquilla and I heard someone across the aisle mention Medellin. I told them I was going to Cartagena. Everyone was enthusiastic and eager to get started and chattered excitedly. However, it was starting to get late and we would be arriving in Colombia sometime the next morning, so we tried to quiet down and get some sleep before waking up in another part of the world. I don't think anyone went right to sleep, though. I know I didn't. I settled back in my seat, trying to imagine what it would be like in Cartagena. Would it be fun? Would I make friends? Would my Spanish be good enough? Where would I live? How many other teachers were there at my school? Would they all be American, or would some be Colombian? So many questions! I prayed before I drifted off to sleep: *Father, be with me in Cartagena; let this be a wonderful adventure, a real fantasy come true. Help me make friends and do a good job teaching. Please keep me safe and protect me from the communists and drug dealers. Thank You, Father, for this wonderful opportunity.*

We arrived in Barranquilla, Colombia around 9:30 the next morning, somewhat dazed and disoriented but snapping out of it fast. Like the others with me, I looked all around, taking in the different sights, sounds and smells of this new country, well, at least, new to me. Since we were in an international airport, however, we saw many people who looked and dressed just like us. Mixed in with them were many shades of brown-skinned women in colorful clothes and men with their *serapes*. I was surprised to hear Spanish and not be able to understand it. There must be many dialects of Spanish in the country, I thought. Would I be able to make myself understood if I couldn't understand what the Colombians said to me?

The other teachers and I said our goodbyes and wished each other good luck. Then we were shuttled off to other planes which would take us to our individual cities, except for the woman who was going to teach in Barranquilla.

The flight to Cartagena was short. I climbed down from the plane into bright sunlight, blistering heat and sauna-like humidity, and I started to perspire immediately. The sky was such a brilliant blue. Some of the men I saw were dressed in business suits and women in professional attire. But most wore their native bright colored clothes and *serapes*. Young people, I noticed, dressed like their Americans counterparts. Beyond the airport I saw stunning trees with red or purple flowers on them and luscious green grass.

I walked slowly into the airport itself and looked around, wondering if someone were going to meet me and how we would recognize each other. Then I noticed an American man and woman holding up a sign with my name on it. What a neat way to be found, I thought, heading toward them. Glancing at others around me, I suddenly felt silly. I was practically the only white, non-Hispanic person getting off the plane! The couple meeting me were the only white, non-Hispanic people among all the various shades of brown-skinned people in the airport! I was sure I was blushing and had a silly smile on my face as I approached them.

When I reached them, the man said, "Hello, you must be Sandy Cone." I nodded. "I'm Dan Burke and this is my wife Helen. I'm the Director of the American Language School."

He was tall (of course, everyone looked tall to me), with longish brown hair, glasses, wearing a white shirt with the sleeves rolled up.

Helen was much shorter than he. She was quite attractive, but she looked hot and uncomfortable in her long-sleeved dress.

While we waited for my suitcases to arrive, Mr. Burke ushered us into a small *cantina,* like a café, in the airport, to get something to drink. The waiter approached, and I prepared myself to order a glass of water in Spanish. But, when he spoke, I couldn't understand him. Mr. Burke answered him, apparently used to the local dialect, and ordered coffee for himself and his wife, then looked at me for my order.

"Agua, por favor," I told the waiter.

Mr. and Mrs. Burke then asked me about my flight down, where I lived in the States, how I heard about the American Language Schools, my education and the like. Mr. Burke also told me about the Cartagena American Language School, but not as much as I wanted to know. I couldn't quite picture what he described. As we rose to go retrieve my luggage, he told me that I would be staying with them until I found an apartment for myself. Helen Burke smiled warmly at me and seemed pleased. Mr. Burke picked up my satchel and we headed for the baggage carousels.

My first suitcase arrived very quickly, but then we waited and waited for the second one. And then we waited some more. When all the luggage had been off-loaded, the men started closing down the carousel. I was dismayed. I hadn't even considered that I would have problems down here in Colombia, let alone one as soon as I arrived!

We traipsed over to the baggage claim office. The man in charge, whose English was fairly good, apologized for the inconvenience and told us that they would do their best to find my missing suitcase as quickly as possible. Possibly, he said, it was still in Barranquilla and would arrive on the next flight, which could be later today. . .or tomorrow. Hopefully, it hadn't gone to another city. He told us we'd be notified immediately when it was found and he wrote down Mr. Burke's phone numbers for his home and the school so he could call him. He went on to explain that once the suitcase was found it would be delivered to a location in the center of town. He wrote the address down on a piece of paper and gave it to Mr. Burke.

"I hope you find it soon," said Mr. Burke. "That's half of her luggage."

"We will do our best, sir."

Grumbling under his breath, Mr. Burke ushered us away from the office and out of the airport to his car. I was thinking to myself that it was only a lost suitcase, but did a problem have to happen on my first day in Cartagena? I told myself it was just a lost suitcase, something that happens all the time. Right? I brushed it off but I did hope they would find it.

Mr. Burke put my suitcase and satchel into the trunk of his car and the three of us drove away from the airport. As I watched eagerly out the window, we seemed to head straight toward the Caribbean. I was intrigued by all the new sights I was seeing. The sky especially caught my attention: it was so blue and clear, not a wisp of a cloud in sight. The grass was such a perfect green, like it got exactly the right amount of water and rain. And the trees had such unusual colored leaves and flowers. Noticing the homes we passed, I watched them get larger and larger. They began to look more and more like mansions, with beautiful gardens and manicured lawns.

As we turned down the street toward the Burke home, I realized it was nearly on the shore of the Caribbean. It was large and beautiful. When we pulled into their driveway and parked, I couldn't help gawking at all the beauty around me. The Caribbean sparkled and shimmered from the sun dancing on the ripples and waves. The grass surrounding the house was lush and thick. The sky over the Caribbean radiated hues from the deepest to the palest of blues. I was awestruck by the beauty. I couldn't help comparing it to Lake Erie, Buffalo's lake, where I grew up. Lake Erie never looked like this!

Then I pivoted and took a good look at their house. "Grand" and "mansion" popped into my mind; the place was huge. It was painted an off-pink with shutters around each window painted a contrasting rust color. Surrounding the house was a veranda rampant with colorful vines and flowers and verdant green plants, like nothing I'd seen in the places I'd lived in the States (of course, that was limited to New York, Pennsylvania and Illinois). Helen Burke was smiling at me when I finally met her eyes.

"I felt the same way when I first got here, too," she told me. "It is very pretty, isn't it?"

"Oh, yes, Mrs. Burke!" I enthused.

"Please, call me Helen."

"Thank you, Helen."

"Well," said Mr. Burke, "let's get Sandy into the house and settled. I still have some things I need to get accomplished today."

I paused at his statement. Was my presence in their home going to be a problem? Maybe he just wasn't impressed by all the beauty around him anymore. Or maybe he was just a very busy man, directing the school and all and needed to get going. Or maybe he just wanted to impress me with how important he was. Who knows what he really meant? Even Helen was looking at him a little funny.

We set my suitcase and satchel down inside the front door and the Burkes gave me a tour of their beautiful, well-appointed home. The art on their walls looked expensive and probably was. They might even have been originals, for all I knew. Many of them depicted scenes of what I presumed was Colombia. All the rooms were tastefully decorated, each with its own theme and color-scheme. They flowed together through graceful archways from one room to the other. We started with their formal parlor which led into a more comfortable-looking living room, then into a dining room with a long graceful table and chairs. From the high ceiling above hung an exquisite chandelier, sparkling like diamonds. From there, we entered the kitchen. It was large as well, well stocked and very organized. A short woman in a maid's uniform stood at the stove and nodded her head at all of us. Helen introduced her as Lolita, their maid, and explained in Spanish who I was to Lolita.

From there, they led me to the back of the house where there were four bedrooms: the master suite where the Burkes slept, two guest bedrooms, and their maid's room. Double doors led onto a back patio and a swimming pool. They showed me which room I would have while I was there. Though I couldn't see the Caribbean through my window, I could clearly hear the waves lapping and slapping against the shore. Turning from the window, I saw that the walls were covered with pink wallpaper with flowers on it. There was a four-poster bed with a decorative pink coverlet on it, a recliner and lamp near the window. In addition, I saw a good-sized dresser, a roomy closet, and a private bathroom. I'd never stayed in a room like this in my life, so grand, so comfortable-looking, and I loved it! Boy, wait until I write Nana and Mom about this!

The Burkes left me to get unpacked and showered. When I went back down the hall toward the kitchen, Helen met me and asked if I'd eaten anything this morning, besides the glass of water at the airport. I told her no, and she went right into the kitchen to Lolita and had her make me a breakfast of scrambled eggs, toast, juice and coffee. I saw that Helen had changed her clothes and was much more comfortable looking. She seemed like a very nice person.

Mr. Burke came into the dining room as I finished eating, looking anxious to be on his way. I thought he was going to let me stay at the house to relax and unwind on my first day. But he surprised me by offering to drive me around Cartagena so I could get a sense of the city, before we went to the school. Then he had a meeting, but he'd be back to pick me up around five.

I was excited as he drove me around the area of Cartagena nearest the Caribbean where many parks and gathering areas were located. I ooh'd and aah'd at the tall palm trees, tropical foliage, colorful plants, and the deep green of the grass. I was so taken in by sights, I nearly missed the wall right in front of me!

Looking up, I got a good look at the massive stones that stretched around Cartagena. I tried to imagine pirates attempting to invade the city and finding themselves unable to surmount the massive walls. They were truly impressive. Many parts of them looked as new and impregnable as they must have looked hundreds of years ago. However, I could see some places where the stone structure was breaking down. Still, it was very imposing, like nothing I'd ever seen before.

From there, we headed in toward the city proper, where I saw brightly painted homes, both stand-alone and apartments joined together, which were a delight to the eyes. It was as if a child had been given a palette with all the possible colors of paint on it, who happily chose the brightest and prettiest of them and painted each building a different color.

But then things seemed to change. The grass and vegetation went from lush green to faded green, then to nothing but brown dirt. The size of the homes shrunk smaller and smaller as well, and almost all the stand alone homes disappeared. Many of the smaller streets weren't even paved. The colors of the houses also changed, fading from bright to washed-out colors as the paint wore off. The condition of this part of the city reminded me of the slums in Chicago and Buffalo. Compared to where the Burkes lived, this area was indeed a slum. Maybe this was the oldest section of town? Had all the rich people, or at least the older, established families who used to live here moved out to the suburbs like they were doing back home?

The other thing that struck me was the trash strewn around the streets and the many large garbage cans overflowing at the curbsides. I could already imagine rats scurrying from one to the other after dark. I also noticed that there were very few cars on the streets. Mr. Burke, sensing my disappointment at what I was seeing, explained that this was the old section of the city and like big old cities around the world, people were moving away from the center of town to nicer, cleaner places where they could live in nicer homes.

We were now entering an old business district and I couldn't understand why. It couldn't be just to see Cartagena's version of a slum. Then I figured it out – this was where the school was located! The school was in the middle of the poorest section of the city. I was expecting to see a stand-alone public-school building with a playground or a basketball court or a football stadium like back home. We turned a corner and there it was, the American Language School, right in the middle of the block. It was just an ordinary rundown building squeezed between other ordinary rundown buildings. All of them were only two stories high. I wondered how such a small building could function as a school. There wouldn't be enough space! (You can tell I grew up in a big-city where even the poorest schools had at least three or four floors and some sort of playground.)

Hopefully, I thought, the school used both floors in the building. However, as we approached it, I saw that the sign for the school also included the names of several businesses in the building. Mr. Burke drove past the school, turned left at the next corner, then left again into the alley behind the school and parked the car. We entered the building by the back door, walked down a dimly-lit hall to the flight of stairs going to the upper floor. I noticed the doors to offices on the first floor were mostly closed and dark. I felt apprehensive as we climbed the stairs to the second floor, not knowing exactly what to expect.

The top of the stairs opened onto a foyer-like area where two desks sat side by side to the left of a closed door that I assumed was Mr. Burke's office. Behind one of the desks sat a very pretty Latina who had olive skin, large, beautiful, dark eyes and dark, wavy hair flowing down her back. She was stunning. Standing next to the second desk was another Latina, much fairer, with hazel eyes and light-colored hair, but just as attractive. Next to them stood three men and another woman. All talking and activity promptly ceased as we reached the landing and everyone was facing us or rather, me. I flushed from all that attention.

Mr. Burke greeted everyone by name, for my benefit I'm sure, and shook hands all around. Then he turned to me with a little flourish and introduced me.

"This is Sandy Cone, our newest teacher from the States," he informed them.

"Cone? Like ice cream cone?" asked the blond American-looking man.

"Yes, vanilla flavor," I replied automatically. He grinned at me and I had to grin back. It broke the ice.

Pointing to him and his wife, Mr. Burke told me, "This is Tom and Jill Hindes, our other two teachers from the States" (Only three of us from the States? Were the two Latino men teachers also? This definitely was a small school!). Tom was still grinning at me. Both he and his wife stepped forward, greeted me warmly and smiled their welcome. They looked like they were glad I was here which was encouraging.

Pointing to the dark-haired Latina sitting at the desk, he said, "This is Rosita, my right-hand assistant. She helps me run this place." Rosita rose from her chair and came forward with a bright smile which really accentuated her beauty and reached out to shake my hand enthusiastically. "So glad to have you here, Sandy Vanilla Cone!" Everyone chuckled, including me.

The other Latina was next. Mr. Burke called her Leona. She was smiling, too, as she came forward and shook my hand. "*Bienvenidos!*" she said. Welcome! Mr. Burke explained that Rosita was his secretary and Leona was secretary for the school.

Then Mr. Burke gestured toward a good-looking dark olive skinned Latino, saying, "And this is Julio, our 'Director of Barrio Activities.'" So he wasn't a teacher, after all. Everyone laughed, slapping him on the back as he came toward me. He paused dramatically, turned toward his friends and bowed, grinning from ear to ear. He was not only handsome, he had an infectious grin and mischief in his eyes. And, if the back-slapping was any indication, he was well-liked. He turned to me and shook my hand, grinning broadly, dimples showing, and stepped back.

"And this," continued Mr. Burke, "is Aurelio, his sidekick!" So only the Hindes and I were the teachers.

"*Si!*" agreed Aurelio. He was tall and robust with a build that reminded me of Superman. His accent wasn't Spanish, though. Spanish was his second language. He looked Italian to me. I shook hands with him as everyone started talking to me at the same time. Most spoke very understandable English, except Leona. I wasn't sure if she knew English at all. Aurelio had his own peculiar accent. But they all were welcoming and friendly and seemed pleased to have me here. So, I thought to myself, this was to be my "school family," the people most involved in my adventure here in Cartagena, Colombia for the next year.

My impression was very positive so far, except for having imagined a much larger institution and many more teachers; but I'd take what I had here with gratefulness. Six pleasant, easy to talk-with new coworkers. I sighed happily. I let the pleasure of meeting these people offset the lost suitcase. I silently thanked God for the warm reception I got here.

"There are two more people," interrupted Mr. Burke, quieting everyone down, "but they aren't here right now. One is Archie, who has helped us with our social programs once a month. He also hangs around here a lot. You'll meet him soon," he said to me. "The other person is Joe Bastien, one of our teachers who has finished his year here and will be returning to the States shortly. He should be back to pick up his last paycheck, if nothing else. You'll be inheriting Joe's classes, Sandy, which Tom and Jill will have until you're ready to teach. Tom and Jill will also be training you, probably starting tomorrow."

Everything seemed so organized. So far, so very good!

Mr. Burke then turned my attention to the rooms surrounding the lobby. He pointed out three classrooms (Tom's, Jill's and *mine*), a library room with Spanish and English books, his office near Rosita's and Leona's desks, a supply room, a clothes closet, a janitor's closet and the bathrooms.

Mr. Burke then steered me past the stairs we came up on and led me down a hall toward the front end of the floor into a little café. There were a few tables and chairs, a little kitchen area, and an enclosed glass case full of cookies, donuts and pastries. Yum! He introduced me to Daisy, the cook. Her English was very good with a pretty lilt to it. When she smiled, which seemed to be all the time, I could see a gold tooth gleaming in the front of her mouth. Mr. Burke glanced at his watch then, noticed the time and hurriedly said his goodbyes to us before dashing away to his meeting. I visited with Daisy for a few minutes before returning to the lobby and the others.

Tom and Jill Hindes cornered me first. We went back to one of the tables to sit and talk. They asked me many of the same questions Mr. Burke had in the airport and I learned they were from Colorado and had taken this teaching fellowship, partly for the fun of it, and partly because they were very concerned about the spread and growth of communism in South America. Both were proud Americans and proud of our democratic way of life. When they first arrived here, they told me, they would go out with Julio and Aurelio to the *barrios*, areas that separated dark-skinned people from the white people, and talk with the people about their impressions and fears about communism. Wherever possible, they encouraged the people to resist communism, which was trying to overthrow or overtake the Colombian government, and instead trust the United States which supported their government. People were receptive to them, but at the same time wary. The Hindes felt that the peoples' restlessness and confusion came primarily from not fully understanding the differences between democracy and communism and, therefore, weren't sure which way to turn. Tom informed me that the communists have been in Colombia since the 1920's, so they've had a long time to terrorize the people and use propaganda to scare them away from the United States.

After our long, serious conversation, I went back out to the lobby and sat down beside Rosita and Leona. Rosita started peppering me with questions right away. She wanted to know all about me, where I lived in the States, did I have a boyfriend, where did I learn Spanish, and so on. She shared her story with me, too. She lived with her parents, but had lived in the States with her *tía*, her aunt, for a couple of years. When her father took ill, she chose to come back home and stay. He has since recovered his health, she said with relief. She currently has a wonderful boyfriend, she confessed shyly (I wasn't surprised to hear that!). Leona sat there with us, saying nothing, but seemed to understand much of what we were saying.

Out of the corner of my eye I could see Julio pacing impatiently, waiting for my conversation with Rosita to end. I excused myself and started toward him.

"I love you!" he blurted out, thrusting his arms out wide as if to embrace me. There was a smattering of giggles from the others while I just stopped in my tracks and stared at him. "I love you, Sandy!" he exclaimed again. I smiled, but didn't know whether to take him seriously or not. Since the others were amused by his antics, I thought it was safe not to take him too seriously. But then, suddenly, he latched onto one of my hands and started kissing it all over! At that I laughed out loud.

"Come and live with me!" he implored me. "I will love you and cherish you!" He thrust his arms outward from his chest in another dramatic gesture.

Aurelio snorted. "You married!"

"You are?" I asked, my voice rising in surprise. I'm sure my eyes widened as well. I quickly pulled my hand away. Married! How was he going to explain that? Julio abruptly turned to Aurelio and scowled, rattling something off to him in Spanish.

Aurelio shrugged, looking offended, but he turned back to me and said, "Y él tiene tres niños!" And he has three children! I sat back in my chair, wanting to burst out laughing again but thought better of it

"Okay," acknowledged Julio, deflated. "Yes, I am married, and, yes, I do have three children. But healthy Latinos have lovers as well as wives!" This time, my mouth dropped open. I couldn't believe he just said that to me! Me, a lover of a married man? Never in my life have I contemplated or imagined such a thing! I certainly wasn't going to start now! Besides, I was no ravishing beauty (like Rosita) who could turn the heads of men, married or unmarried. I was only an average-looking woman. I was already twenty-two – half of my college class was married by the end of their freshman year at eighteen, and a good portion of what was left of my class were engaged or already married before their graduation. I did hope God would place a good man in my path one day, bless our union and bless us with children. But, I didn't think it would happen on my first day in Cartagena, and certainly not with a man already married!

I shook my head no, feeling a mixture of sadness and anger at his pretentious proposal. "I'm sorry, Julio," I told him, keeping my voice cool. "I don't believe in getting involved with a married man. That's not what I want. I'm sure you're a very nice guy but it's not going to happen."

After a moment, to my great relief, he gave a big expansive shrug. "It's okay," he told me smiling cockily. "I'll wait until you're ready!"

"Julio!"

He laughed, "Just joking!"

"Thank goodness!" I breathed a sigh of relief, laughing a little to relieve some of the tension within me. Turning to Aurelio to change the focus of our conversation I asked, "What about you? What's your story?"

Aurelio turned serious. He explained that he and his family had emigrated here from Italy a few years after World War II, because the country was still war-torn, jobs were scarce, and people were still hurting from the devastation of their crops. On top of that, he was slowly going blind from an explosion at the factory where he'd worked. After he got out of the hospital, where he had been treated for some major burns sustained in the explosion, the doctor told his parents of an eye specialist he'd heard about in Colombia who might be able to save Aurelio's sight.

"Was he able to?" I asked hopefully, but Aurelio turned away, which gave me the answer. He looked down at the floor, his shoulders slumping. I felt bad for him, but I didn't want to pity him, because that felt like condescension to me. I could tell he was a proud man and I wanted to honor that.

His eyes still cast down, Aurelio went on. "My blindness is slow process. *Pero*, the day come when I will be totally blind." It occurred to me that it had already been around fifteen years. How much longer would he have his sight?

"It's okay," said Julio soothingly as he placed a hand on Aurelio's shoulder and rubbed it. There was genuine affection in his voice. "We will all take care of you; you're our brother." Aurelio got up abruptly and went into the bathroom, fighting tears. I don't think he wanted to be "taken care of." Julio and I remained sitting there, quietly thinking our own thoughts about Aurelio.

Rosita spoke softly to us from her desk nearby. "Aurelio is such a good man. It really is a shame that he's going blind." Julio nodded and rose from his chair and followed Aurelio into the bathroom. I joined Rosita and Leona by their desks again. I expected Rosita to say more about Aurelio, but she surprised me by saying, "You need to know some things about Archie before he comes by and surprises you."

"Archie? Uh, what do I need to know about Archie?"

"He is a black man. Won't that be a problem for you, a white woman?"

"No. Not really," I replied. "In the neighborhood where I lived in Buffalo, the blacks and whites lived side by side. We all played together. We went to school together. We were best friends. Color didn't matter. Plus, there were also blacks at my college. It's also true that problems were developing between blacks and whites back then but I never personally felt threatened or harassed by them. So, no, I won't have any problem with Archie being black."

"*Bueno!* Archie is as gentle as a lamb, speaks softly and wouldn't harm a bug. You might be interested to know that he's from California and that he's also a defrocked Bahia priest. And, like Julio, he adores women, which is why he got defrocked. But, Sandy, he's also a poet, a photographer, and a composer of songs," she said.

I commented, "Sounds like an interesting person. I'll look forward to meeting him." Rosita and Leona glanced at each other and shifted back to the work they needed to do. I rose from the chair and decided to check out the little school library before Mr. Burke returned.

"Who runs the library?" I asked Rosita, thinking that I could offer to help him or her

"No one at present so if you want to be in charge of the library, it's yours!" Boy, was I thrilled! I'd had years of library experience – well, six years in my Junior and Senior High schools, without pay, of course, but I also worked in the Elmhurst College library for four years and the Elmhurst public library for one year, both for pay. I am also an avid reader and was thrilled to have a place right under my nose to get books. I offered another prayer of thanks to God. The school, the staff, and the library were all positive things, definitely off-setting the lost suitcase. Well, library, here I come!

However! When I went into the library, I saw immediately that there was no order, no rhyme or reason to the way the books were arranged on the shelves or the cards in the card catalog! Nothing was in alphabetical order and English and Spanish books were all mixed together on the shelves. It was almost daunting to think about getting it all organized, but I could actually begin to visualize the steps it would take to accomplish that.

First, separate the English from the Spanish language catalog cards.

Second, divide both groups of cards by authors and titles.

Third, after seeing how messily written the cards were, rewrite all of them. I quickly checked the desk drawers and saw no packages of 3"x5" cards around that I could use to redo them. I'd have to ask Rosita about how to buy more.

Fourth, after completing the catalog cards, tackle the books. That means I'd need to separate the English books from the Spanish first, like I did the catalog cards. Once separated, I could begin the process of coordinating the cards with the books.

Fifth, arrange the English books on the left side of the library, Spanish books on the right.

It would take a long time to do all this, I thought to myself, but I did have a whole year to accomplish it, right? Doing that, along with teaching two classes a day Monday through Friday would definitely equal job security for the whole year!

But, first I went out to speak with Rosita and Leona about money for the 3"x 5" cards. Rosita said the library fell under the administrative side of the school and she could give me the money I needed from petty cash. She proceeded to do so and suggested I go to the *supermercado,* and buy them now.

"Would I have time before Mr. Burke returns?" I asked. Rosita checked the time and nodded yes. "Where exactly is the *supermercado*? How do I get there?" She drew a little map for me and sent me on my way, promising to tell Mr. Burke where I was and that I'd be back soon, if he arrived before I got back.

Eagerly, I set out on my little excursion, my first "little adventure" into Cartagena on my own. I found the *supermercado* with no trouble, thanks to Rosita's map, but got lost in the store, which was large and seemed to be arranged haphazardly. Eventually, I found the right section and the 3"x5" cards I needed. I made my way to the checkout counter, counted out the money carefully, and proudly left the store with my purchase. My first day in Cartagena and I had successfully managed to get around in the city and to buy something all on my own. And to think that, not too many hours ago, I was still on the plane coming down from New York City! Of course, there was still the missing suitcase, but that seemed like a minor bump along the way at this point. I returned before Mr. Burke did.

On the way home with Mr. Burke that evening, I glanced around at some the homes we passed, with their bright colorful paint and profusion of flowers and greens by the doors and on the porches. These homes were attached to each other, but I could tell the people were proud of their appearance because they took time to beautify them so well.

When we arrived at the Burkes' home, Lolita had dinner all ready. It was *arroz con pollo*, one of my favorite meals (I had learned how to cook rice with chicken in Spanish club in high school). Lolita's recipe was very tasty! She offered everyone sodas for dinner, but I wasn't a soda-drinker, so I asked her for a glass of water. Mr. Burke assured me right away that Lolita boiled the water, so it was alright to drink it. I remembered being warned by the doctor who gave me my shots of the absolute necessity to boil the water down here, so I was relieved by Mr. Burke's statement.

Then I thought about how much water I'd drunk at the school all afternoon because of the heat and humidity. When I thought about it, the water had come from the sink faucet. Not boiled water!! Oh, no! Was I going to get ill? I couldn't remember what you got from unboiled water and was too tired to think much about it, to be honest. I didn't know I should have gone to a doctor immediately.

Shortly after dinner, I retired to my bedroom. I hadn't gotten much sleep on the plane coming down, and had spent most of the day driving around Cartagena and visiting the school. Nor was I prepared for the heat and humidity. Buffalo and Elmhurst were far more moderate in temperature (to put it mildly!) All I wanted to do was shower and go to bed. I did want to write my family and Lori and Carol about my first day in Cartagena and do my devotions before going to bed, but I was just so weary. I settled for the shower and crawling into bed. I sunk down under the luxurious soft coverlet and listened to the waves softly crashing against the shore, which I could hear clearly through my open window.

.   .   .

Early the next morning, I peeked out my bedroom door to see if I could hear anyone else up. I turned to see Lolita coming down the hall towards me, carrying an armful of folded towels.

"*Ay, Señorita!*" she gasped.

"What?" I answered in English, forgetting I was supposed to use Spanish.

"*Su cara! Su frente! Su cuello! Sus brazos!*" Your face, your forehead, your neck, your arms!

I quickly looked down at myself. All I could see were my arms – which were covered with large welts everywhere! I felt my face, neck and forehead and there were just as many welts there, too. I hurried into the bathroom to look in the mirror. Everywhere, from the tips of my fingers up to the arms of my pajama top, and from the neckline of my pajamas up to my hairline, was a lumpy mass of what looked like hundreds of mosquito bites. . .all starting to itch like mad! When I came back to the bedroom door, Lolita and Helen were coming toward me, the towels still in Lolita's arms. Helen took me over by the bedroom window so she could see what I looked like in bright light.

"Mosquito bites," she decided after studying me for a moment
I nodded. "That's what I thought, too."
"Stay here. I'll go get some Calamine lotion." She returned a few minutes later, and lathered me up with the lotion: face, neck, chest, arms.
She gave me the tube of lotion and told me to apply it every three to four hours. She left then and I got dressed, trying not to get the lotion all over everything. Feeling uncomfortable, itchy and sticky, I headed hesitantly for the kitchen. Mr. and Mrs. Burke had already started eating their breakfast but Lolita set my plate down in front of me as soon as I sat down.

"*Gracias!*" I told her. She nodded and gave me a shy smile.

Helen looked at me with sympathy, but Mr. Burke took one look and started to grin. I didn't think getting stung by a zillion mosquitos was funny at all! And, despite the Calamine lotion, I was still itchy.

"School day," announced Mr. Burke, getting up from the table a few minutes later, still smiling. I didn't feel like smiling back at him. Nor did I feel like going to the school and have everyone seeing me look like this. But off to school we went, like it or not. How do you hide a bumpy face and arms covered with pink lotion? Clearly this wiped away the fun excursion of yesterday and was worse than my missing suitcase!

"Mr. Burke," I started meekly, but I stopped because I didn't know how to ask a brand new boss for a favor on the first day of a new job. He didn't hear me, apparently, because he turned to me at the same moment and suggested that I work in the library today, so everyone wouldn't be gawking at me and I wouldn't be spreading any germs. Germs? Mosquito bites carried germs? Never mind. I agreed quickly to his splendid idea!

Arriving at the school, I barely gave anyone a chance to say hello to me as I headed straight for the library. I sat at my little desk with my back to the door, which I had pulled nearly closed as I entered, and started idly getting ready to rewrite the catalog cards. For some reason, I didn't feel as excited about it today as I had yesterday. As I looked the cards over, I caught a few mis-alphabetized and I automatically began to put them in order. It's my nature, for good or ill, to organize, straighten things out, file things correctly, have everything in its proper place. So I set to work making sure everything was correct.

"*Hola,*" a soft voice said from the doorway behind me.

I turned around and found Leona standing there, her face registering surprise as she saw all the mosquito bites and Calamine lotion.

"*Qué pasó?*" she asked, coming into the room.

"Mosquito bites. Uh, c*omprende?*"

"*Si.* Yes. *Pobrecita!*"

"*Estoy bien, pero yo. . .*" I'm fine, but I. . .My mind blanked on the word for "itch," so I just said it in English.

"*Yo comprendo,*" she replied, nodding with a concerned look. Leona was a very caring person, I realized. I guessed she was in her early twenties, like me, and I could picture her married to a Prince Charming kind of fellow, with three or four children surrounding her, as well as her parents. She seemed such a quiet, sweet, loving person who should have a large family to mother. As she came further into the library, I saw that others were standing behind her. One by one, they came in to check me out and murmur their condolences, but they all left grinning, like Mr. Burke – probably glad it had happened to me and not them.

After everyone left, I got back to work. I found I had a bit more energy. So, picking up the first messy-looking English catalog card, I began the process of rewriting it and then the next one, and the next one. Soon I had several done and arranged them in piles on my desk. It was mind-soothing work for me and it got my mind off my itchy bites. This was how I began the lengthy process of organizing the library. It would end, I hoped, with an author and title card for each book and each book in its proper place on the shelf.

The piles were growing high on my desk when I eventually came up for air. I sat back in my chair and stretched, then looked down at my small desk and realized I needed more space. The four piles of cards (English author, title; Spanish author, title) were so close together they were spilling off the edges of the desk and I was constantly picking them up. I wondered if Julio or Aurelio could find a card table for me to use. I went out looking for one of them, coming across Aurelio first. He jumped at the chance to "rescue" me. He found an old card table in the supply closet, set it up in the middle of the library and stabilized the wobbly legs. I couldn't thank him enough. Aurelio's English, I thought, wasn't so bad once you got used to the strange accent. I ventured to ask him if, later on, he would help me rearrange the books on the shelves.

"*Pero*, me no read Spanish or English," he told me.

There went my hopes of him helping me. But (picture a light bulb flashing above my head) what if I had all the books arranged in alphabetical order, ready to be shelved? He'd only have to put them on the shelves in the same order as he picked them up. He wouldn't need to be able to read. I mentally patted myself on the back for thinking of such a great solution! I'd talk to him later, when I got closer to the time for doing that.

I decided it was time for a break as a nearby church bell donged the noontime hour. Rosita and Leona came to the library door and asked if I wanted to go to lunch with them.

"Not looking like this," I answered. They both nodded understandingly.

"We'll bring you something back, *si?*"

"*Si*". I smiled my gratitude. "*Gracias!*" They left and I went down to Daisy's to get a drink of water.

"Do you boil the water, Daisy?" I asked her, feeling foolish and anxious at the same time.

"You bet I do!" she responded.

I grinned and relaxed. "May I please have a glass of ice cold water?"

"Coming right up!" Here was the solution to my water problem, I thought with relief. Maybe nothing bad will come from all the water I drank yesterday from the faucet. Maybe. *Please, God?*

I visited with Daisy for a while as I drank my water and learned that she was originally from Cozumel [located on the northern shore of the Caribbean] and had learned some English in school but, mostly, she learned English while working on an American cruise ship as a cook and baker. In fact, she learned German, Polish and Russian, too. She said since the cooks were from all over, she also learned how to cook foods from all over. I found Daisy delightful and easy to be with. She smiled a lot, her gold tooth gleaming.

Rosita and Leona brought me back some rolled tacos with a spicy red sauce to dip them in. The sauce was a too little hot for my taste buds, but otherwise, they sure were good. By the end of the afternoon, I felt like I had made some headway on the catalog cards. It was actually going more smoothly than I expected, although some of the cards were nearly impossible to decipher and I had to go out to Rosita to help me figure them out. Still, I was making progress – not that I expected to get it all done in the next few weeks, of course. But it was encouraging to see the cards in the catalog box growing steadily smaller and the piles on the rickety table growing steadily higher.

Time for another good stretch. I felt satisfied. As I got my nose out of the catalog cards, however, I became aware of my itching face and arms. Time for more lotion. The library, I was convinced, would became my place of refuge, my sanctuary, as it had been all through my school days. I imagined I would come in early each day to work in the library, leaving me time to prepare my lessons and teach later in the day. I didn't meet with Tom and Jill Hindes that day to get trained, as originally planned, because of the pink-lotioned bumps all over the visible parts of me, but they did give me a teacher's guide and student workbook to begin to familiarize myself with the style of teaching they used at the school. I took time to look the books over that evening at the Burkes' home and found them helpful and easy to understand. I thanked God, again, for the friendliness of the staff, the thoughtfulness of the Hindes, and the library. This was going to work out just fine – despite the mosquito bites and my missing suitcase.

The next day, with my face and arms still looking lumpy and pink, Mr. Burke suggested I continue working in the library. Another day of mind-numbing bliss, which I made the most of by plowing through more of the cards, rewriting them, and stacking them on their appropriate piles, which were growing higher and higher. Of course, this was the easy part of revamping the library, although I was getting writer's cramp. It was the reorganization of the books on the shelves that would entail the most physical work and take some time to do. I could tell that Aurelio would be too busy to help me since he was such a strong guy and did most of the grunt work around the school. That meant I'd be doing it all by myself. Oh well, such is life. I wasn't worried about it; I knew I could do it.

That evening, sitting on my bed in the Burkes' guest room, I wrote what I hoped was an amusing letter to my folks and my college friends about the lost suitcase, the mosquito bites and shopping at the *supermercado*. I made light of the fact that my suitcase hadn't been located yet, celebrated that the bites were beginning to fade, and enthused about my shopping adventure. I hoped I assured everyone that I was doing fine down here and enjoyed staying with the Burkes in their beautiful home. I even mentioned Julio's "proposal" and described everyone at the school. I enthused about the library and what I was trying to accomplish there. I didn't mention how homesick I was, though, because, as exciting and different as everything was here in Cartagena, it wasn't home and I wasn't surrounded by family and friends.

I arrived at the school the next morning, Thursday, greeted everyone and headed for the library. The mosquito bites, I was happy to notice, were nicely fading away and I didn't itch as much.

Mr. Burke and the Hindes approached me about mid-morning and Mr. Burke informed me that the Hindes would start training me today. Included in the training, Tom told me, was sitting in on their classes this afternoon and tomorrow afternoon. All week, I thought, my energies had been invested in the library where I was very comfortable getting it organized and operational.

However, I did hire on as a teacher, not a librarian, so I agreed readily to the training. Mr. Burke left and the Hindes ushered me down to Daisy's Corner (their pet name for it), where we got some coffee, a donut each, and settled at one of the tables.

We went over lesson plans and Tom emphasized that the first week and most of the second week of the three-month course were taught all in Spanish. Gradually, as the students' English vocabulary increased, we would use more and more English in class, until, at the end, everyone was speaking English as fluently as they possibly could. He reminded me that the first week of classes would be over tomorrow; Monday started the second week. I began to get caught up in their enthusiasm, plus I loved listening to them talk so fluently in Spanish – when they suddenly started speaking to me *only* in Spanish and made me respond only in Spanish! It felt like a test of some sort, and, they informed me afterwards, it was! Jill and Tom grinned at me, patted my back and told me I had passed!

"Whew!" I exclaimed, feeling the heat in my face. "You really caught me off guard! I sure wasn't expecting that!"

"We know," said Jill, smiling broadly. "But you did just fine. That's how it's done with all the new teachers coming here, including us."

"Our first class starts at 4:00 pm, the second at 6:30 pm," explained Tom. "They go for two hours each, and we have a short break in between classes to catch our breath. Why don't you sit in on my 4:00 and Jill's 6:30 this afternoon? Then, tomorrow, her 4:00 and my 6:30. That way you'll get to meet all the students and you'll get a feel for the way we teach, and how we try to match our teaching with the needs of the students."

"Sounds perfect!" I agreed excitedly.

Back in the library, I looked over the teacher's guide and student workbook again, this time with a clearer picture in my mind. I hoped this would turn out to be a learning, growing, fun time for the students – I knew it would be for me. I have to admit I was a little apprehensive that I'd get tongue-tied in my first class on Monday, or stumble over words I know so well, or simply go blank. Gulp! *Help me, Lord!* I put the textbooks aside and turned back to the card catalog. That calmed me down. I let myself become engrossed again, working diligently on the cards and gradually made some headway.

Several of the cards, I noted unhappily, were simply too illegible to decipher, even with Rosita's and Leona's help. I set them aside. After I united all the rest of the cards with their books, I would be able to find what books the cards might go with. But the piles of rewritten cards on the card table were proof that I was progressing right along.

Mr. Burke came to the library door just then and announced that my missing suitcase had been found! It was waiting for me at the Luggage Shack downtown and he'd be free in an hour to take me over there. I thanked him. I was really surprised that it'd been found, figuring it was gone forever. I was planning on buying a couple of replacement outfits when I started getting my paychecks.

. . .

We finally left to go to the Luggage Shack. I wasn't sure what to expect with a name like that. When I saw it, I understood. It looked like a shack, alright, but it was actually a very small building that was crumbling and falling apart. There was no door, only a curtain which looked like it had never been washed and only partially covered the opening. When Mr. Burke stopped the car, he told me he had to take off for a meeting but, when I was done, to call a taxi to return to the school. I nodded my understanding.

I walked tentatively up to the curtain. There was no light on inside and part of me wanted to forget the whole thing. But, after taking a deep breath for courage, I pushed the curtain back and stepped hesitantly inside. The tiny one room building was so hot and stuffy inside I could hardly breath. My eyes didn't adjust to the dimness very quickly but my nose worked just fine. I could smell the man in the darkness in front of me. He reeked of cigar smoke and another smell, too, kind of sweet (Marijuana?). He also smelled of urine and body odor. On top of that, his breathing was heavy, like that of a large man who was winded. I noticed a little window above his head, but it had no glass, just a lattice-like grate over it. The taller building next door blocked the sunlight, so even though the place got some meager ventilation, very little light came through. The man was cast in shadows. He seemed massive. Gradually, my eyes began to adjust.

"Passport," said the man in heavily-accented English. How could he tell I was American, I wondered? I hadn't said a word yet. Did my clothes – which I'm sure he could barely see in the darkness – give me away?

I handed him my passport. He glanced at it, then reached behind his chair where several suitcases were lined up and retrieved mine. How on earth could he tell which one was mine without any light? Did he have super-human vision? Looking up at me, he explained in his broken English that I was to give him a "tip." I rummaged in my satchel for a couple of American dollars, thinking he'd like that over *pesos,* Colombian currency. He looked me in the eye and grinned. It seemed more like a leer to me, causing me to hesitate, which gave him enough time to put his hand on top of mine and clamp it down!

"No, *Señorita,* not that kind," he murmured seductively. "You!" His leer got uglier, his eyes brighter, his smell more nauseating. I was stunned and I just stared at him, comprehending but not believing it.

He took advantage of my hesitation and grabbed my wrist and pulled me closer to him and quickly started to force his other hand up my blouse and under my bra. That snapped me out of my paralysis, and I tried to push him away with my free hand. Did I mention the man probably weighed 300+ lbs.? I definitely was no match for him! He was strong, but I was incensed by his behavior and my Italian stubborn streak rose to the surface. I felt like a volcano about to erupt! I struggled against him with all my might, but he kept his stranglehold on my wrist and kept trying to pull my blouse off. The harder I fought, the more he grinned with excitement. Though he was trembling, from exertion or adrenalin, I don't know, his grip remained like iron, squeezing my wrist until I felt it tingling. The only thing I could think to do was to kick him as hard as possible in the shins, which I did. He grunted in surprise but he didn't let go! I kicked at him again, but he shifted and twisted my arm at the same time. Getting scared then, I screamed for help.

"Help! Help me! Somebody help me!" I yelled at the top of my lungs. In English. Where was my Spanish when I needed it?

At just that moment, a couple of older ladies were passing by the Luggage Shack. They stopped (thank God!) and yanked the curtain open to see what was going on. They stared at the Luggage Man and saw where his hand was. In shock and anger, they yelled at him in loud, scolding voices, mother voices scolding a naughty child. I'm sure everyone on the street could hear them. In fact two or three people slowed down to see what was happening. I'm not sure exactly what the women said to the Luggage Man, but it made him let go of me. I quickly backed away from him, shaking my wrist to get circulation going again and tried to right my messed-up blouse and bra as best as I could. The man, I saw, continued to grin at all of us. He slowly shrugged his big shoulders as if to say, "I'm only doing what comes naturally."

The ladies stood there with arms folded across their chests, glaring at the man, while I grabbed my suitcase, thanked the ladies profusely in Spanish, and ran out of there. I forgot all about calling a taxi in my haste to get away. When I did think of it, I wasn't exactly sure how I would have done it, since there'd been no phone in the shack or anywhere else nearby that I could see.

I started out walking very, very fast to get as far away as possible from the man, then slower and slower as I got tired and overheated. And lost. I had no idea where I was. I finally asked for directions to the school and found out I still had a long way to go. Trudging onward, exhausted and angry at the Luggage Man, I barely saw the bright yellow-painted homes I passed on my way back to the school or the beautiful flowers on their window ledges and porch railings.

I stared straight ahead as I slowly chugged along, seeing nothing but the next street I had to cross to get back to the school. I was afraid I would collapse from heat exhaustion before I got there. Almost an hour later, I arrived at the school, my mouth dry as a bone and the rest of me dripping with perspiration. I dropped my suitcase at the foot of the stairs and went up to the lobby, dropping onto the first chair I came to. Aurelio, standing by Leona's desk, took one look at me and hurried to get me a big glass of water. He got it from the faucet, which didn't even register with me at the time because I so desperately needed something to drink.

I gulped the whole glass down and Aurelio quickly brought me a second glass. I was so grateful and thanked him. Everyone present was standing around me by then, concerned about what had happened. Rosita pulled her chair over and sat by me. She was frowning. "Sandy," she whispered in my ear, "your blouse is torn and smudged." She handed me a hanky to dry my face.

I had planned to say nothing about what the Luggage Man had done, but her concern on top of my exhaustion undid me and I started to cry. I told her what he had tried to do and how the two ladies saved me. Leona, Julio, Aurelio and the Hindes listened with growing anger on their faces. They all murmured kind and caring words to me, massaged my shoulders, and brushed my damp hair off my forehead. Rosita and Leona put their arms around me and hugged me protectively. Aurelio was ready to go over there and "teach the man a lesson." Julio was ready to join him. The men declared that women were meant to be loved, pampered and cared for tenderly, not hurt or raped. (Thank God that man hadn't got *that* far, I thought with a shudder). I closed my eyes and tried to relax, feeling blessed to be among these people at this moment in time. Slowly I began to relax and I felt my heart rate returning to normal.

When Mr. Burke got back from his meeting, everyone rushed to tell him about what the man in the Luggage Shack had tried to do to me. Mr. Burke was appalled and became solicitous.

"Do you need to go home?" he asked.

Part of me dearly wanted to say yes, because I felt so dirty where that man had touched me, but I told him no because I wanted to sit in on Tom and Jill's classes a couple of hours from now. I have to admit that I wasn't naïve about men like the Luggage Man. I had a childhood history of encounters with such men. So, I was knowledgeable. But that didn't mean I expected it to happen to me again. The experience brought back feelings of fear and outrage in me that I thought were long buried.

As these good folks around me drifted back to their work, I found myself reflecting silently that what happened today made a lost suitcase and mosquito bites seem trivial. If those two women hadn't come at the precise moment they did, I would have been raped. I know that sounds like I'm overreacting to what happened at the Luggage Shack, but that man would certainly have overpowered me, and raping me was definitely on his mind. He was so brazen, apparently not caring or worrying about someone else coming to the shack for a suitcase to interrupt him. Without help, I wouldn't have been able to fight him off or stop him. I shuddered, overwhelmed with old feelings of powerlessness and fear.

In the lady's room, I splashed cool water on my face and tried to pull myself together. Looking in the mirror, I used my fingers to pat my hair back into place and wiped my glasses. Taking several deep breaths, I left the bathroom and retreated to the library.

Well, I thought, as I settled at my desk, at least one good thing came out of this mess: I got my lost suitcase back. No, I corrected myself immediately, there were two good things: the suitcase and the two ladies who didn't know me, yet came to my rescue. Then, I stopped myself again, chagrined. I also had to acknowledge the wonderful support I got from my friends here at the school who didn't defend or minimalize what the man did, but believed me and became angry on my behalf. That's true friendship and I marveled at it!

When I was a child and dared tell someone when these kinds of things happened to me, Nana was the only one who believed me. There were no agencies in place to protect children or deal with their abusers in the 1940's and 50's. Even Nana was at a loss about what to do and advised me to keep quiet about it while she hugged me and held me close and tried to comfort me. Apart from Nana in the past, the staff at the school here were the first to believe me and be supportive. I bowed my head and prayed.

As tears sprang to my eyes, I fervently prayed: *Accept my heartfelt thanks O Lord. I am so grateful for Nana's support and belief in me years ago and for these good people here who stood up for me. And thank you for two strong, angry ladies who came to my aid at the Luggage Shack. This has been a traumatic week, O Lord. But everything has turned out okay in the end. I got my suitcase back, my mosquito bites are fading, and the Luggage Man wasn't able to rape me or hurt me more than he did. Please, Lord, let this be the end of my troubles. Let the rest*

of my time here in Colombia be filled with events that bring sunshine and
happiness to my life, filling me with positive memories for when I return
home. Thank you for being present with me, always.

Sighing, I felt my equilibrium returning as a sense of relief washed
over me. God was still in control.

When 4:00 rolled around, I was ready for Tom's class. I was so
impressed watching how he taught, I forgot all about my troubles. He
seemed to know instinctively what his students needed and worked
answers and suggestions into the lesson to address those needs. He
praised them and encouraged them and it was clear they were truly
motivated to learn. After sitting in on Jill's class at 6:30 and seeing how
everyone was totally attentive to her, listening carefully and responding
confidently, I was glad I had decided to stay for this part of the training. I
felt sure that after visiting their classrooms again tomorrow evening, I
would be ready to teach my own classes on Monday. Despite how
grubby and dirty I felt from my encounter with the Luggage Man, I was
glad I had chosen to stay for their classes.

That night at the Burkes, before unpacking my lost-and-found-again
suitcase, I took a long soaking bath to get rid of the lingering effects of
that morning's unpleasantness, and to check my breast and wrist for any
bruises. There they were on my breast, very visible, already green and
getting darker. My wrist, where he had grabbed me and nearly choked
off the blood supply, was already blue and purple in color.

Helen knocked on my door as I was getting dressed for bed. "May I
come in?" she asked. I opened the door for her and she entered, then
motioned me over to the bed and sat down with me.

"Sandy, Dan told me about what happened to you today at the
Luggage Shack. I am so sorry! Are you alright? Did he hurt you?" Her
eyes were filled with such concern that I found myself wanting to
unburden myself all over again.

"Just my one breast and my wrist," I told her softly. "He left
bruises, but he didn't get to do anything more because I screamed for help
and two wonderful ladies stopped and gave him the evil eye. He let go of
me and I ran out of there." Her eyes were brimming with tears for me so
I started to tear up, too. She looked down at my bruised wrist and gently
stroked it. Then she pulled me toward her and hugged me. It felt
wonderful. We hugged a long time and I sensed she had been a victim,
too, in her past. When we separated, she kissed me on the cheek and left.

I knew I would survive this incident, as I did the ones from my childhood. I also knew I needed help doing it. When Helen left, I picked up my Bible, sat in the comfortable chair by the window and, with the rhythmic waves of the Caribbean as a backdrop, turned to Psalm 23:

"The Lord is my shepherd; I shall not want. He makes me lie down in green pastures; he leads me beside still waters; he restores my soul. He leads me in the right paths for his name's sake. Even though I walk through the darkest valley, I fear no evil; for you are with me; your rod and your staff – they comfort me. You prepare a table before me in the presence of my enemies; you anoint my head with oil; my cup overflows. Surely goodness and mercy shall follow me all the days of my life, and I shall dwell in the house of the Lord my whole life long."

Such familiar, inspiring words! Then in Psalm 27, I read these words:

"The Lord is my light and salvation; whom shall I fear? The Lord is the stronghold of my life; of whom shall I be afraid?"

And finally in Psalm 31, these words spoke to me:

"In you, O Lord, I seek refuge. . .You are indeed my rock and fortress; for thy name's sake lead me and guide me."

I let the inspiring faith of a shepherd boy named David, who later became a mighty king and authored most the Psalms, fill me with his trust and confidence in such a magnanimous God.

I do not believe God sends calamity on His people, generates hate and hostility between brothers, makes bad experiences happen to innocent children, or deliberately sends natural disasters on His people to ruin their lives or punish them. I do believe He walks with us through all our life experiences, both good and bad, and gives us the strength, fortitude and perseverance we need to get through them. I felt God's presence at that moment, surrounding me, filling me, assuring me of His love. I know there will come a day of judgment for all of us and those who have harmed others, especially children, will experience God's wrath. As I relinquished my anger at the Luggage Man – just as I had relinquished my anger at those others from my past – I felt God's peace settle on me like a comforting hand. A burden lifted from my heart. I felt lighter and freer.

I sat there for a long time remembering how God had come to me all through my life. The first time was when I was about eight years old. I was walking home from school after telling the school counselor about one of the "incidents" that had occurred to me and getting no help from her. Though I saw sadness in her eyes for me, she silently shook her head indicating there was nothing she could do to help me. As I moped along the sidewalk, I became aware that someone was calling my name. I stopped and looked all around but there wasn't any one on the sidewalk in either direction. Though a little confused by this, I started walking again, wondering if the voice would call my name again. A few minutes later, I heard it. Again, I stopped and looked around. Again, I saw no one. I looked up and down the street trying to figure out where the voice was coming from. It seemed to be as close as the air I breathed. Sighing, I started slowly walking home again, but on high alert now for the next call. When I heard it, I looked straight up to Heaven. My child's heart knew it was God Himself calling! I smiled up at Him, then, thrilled to have solved the mystery of where the voice was coming from. I waved my hand hello to God and a wonderful feeling of peace settled over me like a soft baby blanket. I knew in my heart that God was aware of the incidents that were happening to me and was telling me He knew about them and would always stay near me.

I remembered also a time following another incident when I was hurting and tensed up and had a hard time going to sleep. As I tossed and turned in my bed, I became aware of footsteps walking from our apartment door, through the kitchen where the floor creaked, toward my bedroom which was off to the side of the living room. A curtain separated the living room and bedroom but it was open. The footsteps stopped at that opening and I looked over to see who was there. I was afraid, worrying it might be George, my Mom's new boyfriend who was a drunk.

As I stared at the figure by the curtain, I relaxed; it wasn't George. It was a man, though, but he was indistinct, as if a shimmering see-through cloth prevented me from seeing him clearly. I blinked several times and pinched my arm to make sure I was awake, that he was really standing there.

He was looking directly at me. There was a light over his head and he was dressed in a robe like Jesus used to wear in the pictures in my church – in fact, he reminded me of one particular picture where Jesus had that light above His head and looked out at everyone with love and peace in His eyes. Suddenly, I knew that the man looking at me was

Jesus Himself! He spoke to me, like God did a few weeks before, and told me that He loved me and would always be with me. Then He slowly raised His arm toward me, palm extended, and a warm, peaceful feeling descended upon me and took all my tension away. I snuggled down in bed and went to sleep, feeling loved, protected, and knowing that I was not alone. God never left me after that. He has provided constant comfort and support every day since then.

Now, as in my childhood, the same blanket of peace descended gently upon me, and I went to bed to the sound of the rhythmic waves of the sea rushing forward and retreating; and the assurance that God was still present with me.

. . .

The next morning I woke up and realized it was pay day. I looked forward to it, but wondered how much it would be since I'd only been here five days and those had been spent in the library, thanks to the mosquito bites. When I received my check, I shouldn't have been disappointed, but I was. Mr. Burke was obviously very rigid about no work, no pay. I had worked in the library, though, and I felt I was doing a reasonably good job in there. Mr. Burke, however, had never commented on my working in there or what I was trying to accomplish.

Did he ever compliment anyone here for the work they were doing? I thought back to Monday and his introduction of the staff to me. He obviously liked Julio and Rosita – not that he said anything bad about the others. It was more the tone of his voice. Oh well. My next paycheck should be better so I dismissed the negative thoughts from my mind and went on about my work in the library.

Later that day I sat in on Jill's 4:00 class first and was again impressed with her teaching abilities. She was so smooth that it was clear why her students adored her. Lovely to look at, cheerful and outgoing, she was a great teacher and super-fluent in Spanish. She was an inspiration to me! She told me during the break that she had lived with her family for several years in Belize, a country on the eastern coast of Central America. That explained her proficiency in Spanish. Tom's class went just as well as yesterday's had. He was so professional. I could picture him teaching Spanish in a university in the States, whipping brand new teachers into shape, encouraging them, quietly correcting them or making suggestions. What a natural teacher he was and what a great couple he and Jill made!

Finally, it was the weekend. I spent my time reading, swimming in the Burkes' pool, and resting a lot. Helen and I spent time together, getting to know each other more. She was really a sweet lady. I also straightened my room, made my bed, and collected my dirty laundry. I headed for the laundry room, but Lolita stopped me and insisted that that was her job. I let her take the small load from me as I thanked her. She nodded, smiling her shy smile at me again.

By Monday, I was ready to get back to school. I was feeling much better. The welts and itching from the mosquitos were nearly gone. I took a lunch break with the others at noon and we went to a *restaurante* down the street, where I had a *bifsteak* dinner, which consisted of chopped beef steak, potatoes and vegetables. While eating, I found myself listening to Julio's and Aurelio's account of their visit to a *barrio* this past Saturday.

"The people served mango juice to us and fed us *carnitas y frutos,* various meats and fruit. Half the town came out for the movies, kids and dogs, too. We had a great time!" enthused Julio.

"How often do you go out?" I asked.

"Nearly every Saturday."

"Could I come with you sometime?"

"*Si,* if it's okay with Mr. Burke, it's okay with us," Aurelio answered. I remembered that the Hindes had traveled with them on several occasions when they first arrived, too.

"We'll talk to Burke," Julio assured me. "I'm sure he'll agree, but there's no rush. We go almost every weekend, and you'll be here a whole year."

"True," I said. "And thank you."

Julio then explained how they set up their projector and screen in the town square, or a building if the *barrio* had one, and showed one long and two or three short films. Sometimes, if the little towns were able, they served drinks and maybe some fruit or a snack. Most of the barrios were very poor and were simply grateful to see the films. There was always one film which showed the people how a democracy worked or promoted democratic ideals. There was usually a light, funny Hollywood movie, with subtitles, to entertain them, plus a film about better ways to farm and a cartoon for the children. The goal, besides pushing democracy, was to promote good will and help the people feel like they're part of the larger world. Their happiness and gratitude were the only "refreshments" Julio and Aurelio often received, but it was enough. After hearing all of that, I was eager to join them and experience it for myself.

That afternoon, I met Archie, one of the two men not present last Monday when I arrived. He was as Rosita described him. Very dark but not very tall, with square glasses perched low on his nose. Hanging on his shoulder was a black leather camera bag. He had the softest voice when he said hello to me. I'd really have to listen carefully if I wanted to catch everything he said. For a minute or two, he just stood and studied me. It felt like he was sizing me up.

"Do you want to ask me something?" I said to him.

Archie smiled. "No," he replied, "I'll wait until I get to know you better. Do you have questions for me?" he asked, sitting down.

"Yes. Mr. Burke and Rosita told me about you and I've been waiting to meet you. My question is, are you a professional photographer? I heard you were very good at it, as well as a composer of songs and a poet."

He smiled, pleased at the praise. "No, I'm just an amateur photographer," he answered, "but I love to take pictures of the Colombian people, of people of all kinds. I also do sunrises, sunsets and scenery. . .as well as beautiful women." He paused, then asked in a quiet, serious voice, "Does the color of my skin bother you?"

"Not at all," I promptly assured him. He cocked his head, considering, then nodded his approval.

"I understand you put on monthly programs here," I commented. "I was told there was entertainment or speakers or discussion groups at these programs. Right?"

"I have in the past, yes," replied Archie slowly. "I wanted to encourage Burke to provide a variety of experiences for the school to share with the community, to increase awareness of the school and bring in more students. He was reluctant at first, but warmed up to the idea, with Rosita's help, I might add."

"You don't do it anymore?"

"Burke doesn't seem to be as interested as he used to be," he said carefully.

Hmmm, I thought, but said, "It sounds like something I would have enjoyed."

He considered that, then said," I don't think I can get Burke to hold another program. He seems to be too busy to talk about it when I approach him." He stood up then, and paused before speaking again, which I gathered was his style, and added quietly, "I'd like to visit with you some more some time, if that's okay with you."

"Of course," I told him without hesitation, delighted to have a chance to get to know this man more.

As he left, I thought about how different he was from Julio and Aurelio, and not only in the color of his skin. He was more serious-minded, for one thing. As a photographer, he probably had an artistic eye and wasn't as good at doing things around the school with his hands like Julio and Aurelio were. I thought of the way he studied me. What was he thinking about? Anyway, he was an interesting addition to the group here.

Finally, that afternoon, I met the students in my 4:00 class. I recognized most of them from Tom's and Jill's classes. Now they were my students! I remembered that my lessons were to be all in Spanish until Thursday or Friday.

I looked around at everyone who had quickly and quietly taken their seats and who were now watching me expectantly. I saw that there was a wide range in ages, from one child of about eight or so to an older white-haired gentleman, with all the other men and women (mostly women) falling in between.. I reminded myself that this was a special school, reaching out to anyone in the community who wanted to learn English.

I had decided to spend the first couple of days getting to know my students and finding out how much English they already knew and what they had the most trouble with. I began by telling them about myself.

"*Hola, clase, buenas tardes. Yo soy Señorita Sandy Cone, su maestra.*" Hello, class, good afternoon. I am Miss Sandy Cone, your teacher. Before I could go any further, the young boy spoke up.

"*Por favor, Señorita, en inglés.*" Please, Miss, in English.

"*En inglés?*"

"*Si!*" Other students chimed in their agreement with the boy. So I told my story in English, ending with why I came to Cartagena, which was because I wanted to help all of them learn as much English as they could, so if they had an opportunity to go to the States, they'd be prepared. I repeated what I said in Spanish for those who didn't understand enough English yet.

Cheers went up around the room. I felt like we were off to a good start. However, now it was their turn.

I began by asking each student to stand and tell his or her name, age (if they wanted to) and why they wanted to learn English. The young boy jumped up immediately and bowed. He introduced himself in English, to my surprise and delight.

"I am Roberto, I have ten years and I study English because I want to move to America. If you, um, adopt? me, I will be your son forever!" He smiled charmingly, or was it ingratiatingly? Then he came forward, bowed again, and kissed my hand! I gave him a hug because he was so very cute.

"You adopt me, yes?" he asked, nodding his head and looking hopeful. I smiled down at this waif of a child and told him I wished I could, but I couldn't. His smile faltered and the brightness faded in his eyes and I immediately felt sad for bursting his bubble. If I were older and richer, I would have adopted him in a heartbeat! Instead, I asked him about his parents. He told me they had died five years ago, and that his *tía* was like a mother to him. I hugged him again, but became aware that I had been ignoring the other students for too long and sent Roberto back to his seat.

After Roberto's bravery, a number of others also introduced themselves in English, giving their name, their age (or not) and their reason for learning English. Many surprised me by mentioning they wanted to move to America because of the unrest in their country caused by the drug cartels and the communists. They wanted a better, safer life. I wondered how many would actually make it to America.

The old man stood up for his turn. He was quiet-spoken and with a good-enough command of English. He gave his name as Pedro Gonzalez and admitted he was "eighty and two". He said he simply wanted to go to America so he could die there, because God told him America was the Promised Land (as Canaan had been in the Old Testament: God gave Canaan to the Israelites, a land that flowed *"with milk and honey"* Numbers 13:27). Pedro believed God had promised him he would be able to die in America. I didn't know what to say to him, whether to be falsely optimistic about his chances of getting there or to be honest and squelch his faith. Taking the easy way out, I simply told him I hoped his dream came true.

I thanked everyone for telling me about themselves. Now I had to concentrate on finding out what they knew about grammar, nouns, verbs, prepositions, pronouns, possessives and the like. Obviously, a few of the students were pretty advanced, but others were at the beginning. Well, the first lessons were in Spanish anyway so I could begin to help them.

My second class that evening was similar in nature. A few introduced themselves in English, most preferred Spanish. We got to know each other, and I found myself feeling proud of what the students had accomplished in learning some English on their own before coming to this American government-sponsored Language School. Many had learned English in school, several in the workplace, others in American homes where they served as maids. I was inspired by the time and energy they were willing to expend to learn more English.

By 8:30 pm, as the students left class and disappeared down the stairs, I felt my energy level sinking, at least my mental acuity. That had been a lot of hard work! I hadn't spoken that much Spanish during a four-hour period of time, ever.

Nor had I realized how many people yearned to immigrate to the United States to have a better life. True, many had seen American movies and fell in love with all the beautiful people in them and the beautiful homes they saw. I wondered if they believed everyone in America was good looking and rich? Well, I was an American and I wished I was good-looking and rich, too! Most of us are just ordinary-looking people trying to make a life for ourselves. Of all of us at the school here, the best-looking ones were Julio and Rosita and they were two of their own. But I didn't think they were rich and lived in beautiful homes, like the Burkes did.

The next night I decided to play a game with my classes after their lesson. I explained in Spanish, "We're going to go in order around the room, with the first person telling his name, then the next person telling his name, *plus* the name of the person before him. The next person would say his name, then the *two* names of the people before him, and so on." I heard mock groans of agony, but there were smiles and giggles, too, and looks that told me they were up to the challenge.

"In English or Spanish?" asked Roberto.

"Whichever you want," I answered. Everyone sat up a little straighter, looking around and calculating how many names they knew already. "Okay, I'll begin," I said. *"Hola, me llama Señorita Sandy."* Then I pointed to Roberto.

He stood up. "Hello, my name is Roberto, and you are Miss Sandy," pointing at me.

I nodded my approval and pointed to the next person. She stood and said, "My name is Verónica, and you are Roberto (pointing to him), and you are Miss Sandy (pointing to me)." Smiling impishly, she sat back down. As we got to each person, it got more and more difficult, of course, because the list of names kept growing. But everyone was good-natured about helping each other out. When the last person finished, all eyes turned to me in anticipation.

Now it was my turn to name all of them! I knew I wasn't going to get them all right but I really tried. Everyone pitched in to help me out, though, and giggles and laughter erupted around the room at some of my mispronunciations. We all had a good time in the process, so I guess it worked out fine.

"Buen trabajo, Señorita!" Good work, Miss! several commented as class broke up. Everyone was chattering away about the game and who got the most names right as they hurried down the stairs and headed home.

Tom and Jill were standing in the lobby as I came out of the classroom. "Sounds like everyone had a good time in there," commented Tom, grinning.

"Yes, we sure did! I'm going to love teaching here! Thanks for all your help! My classes aren't going to be as coordinated or smooth as yours, but I hope we continue to have as much fun as we've had these last two nights – as well as learn English, of course!"

Tom, Jill and I had a good laugh.

That night as I was getting ready for bed, I reflected on my classes. I knew I shouldn't feel pride in how well the classes went, but I did. They were so eager to learn and responded so well to me. But a tiny, little voice inside me said, *"Humble yourself. Remember, God has given you the gifts of language, this opportunity to teach, and many students yearning to learn enough English to qualify as bi-lingual. Give thanks to God and be grateful."* Obeying that tiny, quiet voice, I knelt at my bed and thanked God. How blessed I felt!

Culture, Communism And Christianity

Two days later, Joe Bastien, the second missing person from my original introductions, came by the school. The others had told me that something had upset Joe just before he took off two weeks ago but no one seemed to know what it was. He just left school before his classes and didn't show up again until today. Joe nodded at everyone as he reached the landing and they all stood up excitedly at the sight of him. But he didn't stop to greet them; he just headed straight for Mr. Burke's office. I was standing in the library doorway, about to get a cup of coffee from Daisy. Rosita beckoned me over and we joined the others who were standing by Mr. Burke's office door to hear what Joe had to say.

"I'll be leaving for the States next week," Joe announced to Mr. Burke. "I came by for my last check. I was also wondering about the new teacher, who should have arrived by now." He stopped and turned around, searching for that new teacher, his eyes finally landing on me. Everyone parted as he came toward me and stretched out his hand. "Hi," he said with a friendly smile. "I'm Joe Bastien. Sorry I'm leaving just as you're arriving. But I, uh, sort of have a proposition for you." I caught eyebrows rising on those listening at the door. Their curiosity at the kind of proposition Joe Bastien would be offering a new teacher he hadn't even met yet was obvious. I thought of Julio's proposition on my first day here and feared this might be the same. I almost groaned out loud, but I swallowed the groan and grinned instead, just as curious as the others.

"I'm Sandy," I said, shaking his hand. "Pleased to meet you. Uh, what kind of proposition are you talking about?"

He blushed suddenly, aware of how that sounded. "Um," he stammered, "I was kind of thinking as I started to pack that you might like a small apartment to live in while you look for another one that you like better. I expected another guy to replace me, because my small apartment is kind of like a bachelor pad. But you could pretty it up, I guess, and make it more suitable for a gal." His blush deepened. He took a deep breath and continued doggedly. "It does have its own bath and some of the greatest neighbors you'd ever want to meet." I noticed smiles on the faces around me. Joe did, too, shrugged and grinned sheepishly.

I also saw Mr. Burke brighten at Joe's suggestion, and I sensed that he was getting tired of having me at his house. I'd been there ten days now and there'd been the business with the lost suitcase and the mosquitos, and not being able to teach my classes right away, and then the Luggage Man incident occurred, so maybe I'd been too much trouble for him. Unaware of my mental ramblings, Joe went on to explain to me that he had a cot, a table and chair and a hot plate, all of which he would leave for me, if I wanted them. He added that he also had a table setting for one, plus a couple of pots.

"How small is your apartment?" I asked.

"Basically one room and the bathroom."

"Oh," I said. Only one room, probably like a dorm room, I thought. Oh, dear. Was that what I wanted? But if Mr. Burke were getting tired of me and Joe's apartment would be just a stop-gap measure until I found a little bigger apartment, then maybe it would work out alright.

Mr. Burke stood up. "Do you want to take her over there now and show it to her, Joe?"

"Sure," he said, then turned back to me. "It's kind of messy, but if you don't mind, it's not a problem for me."

"That's not a problem for me, either."

"Great!" he responded. "Let me get a cup of coffee and one of Daisy's donuts and I'll be ready to go. Join me?" he asked. I nodded okay. Joe and I traipsed back to Daisy's Corner with everyone following behind. They began asking him lots of questions before we even started down the hall.

"Hold on," he told them. "Let me get my coffee, first."

Daisy threw her arms around Joe's neck as soon as she saw him, grinning happily, gold tooth gleaming. He planted a kiss on her cheek. He placed his order and mine, and we gravitated to a table. The others drew chairs around us and could hardly wait to start their questioning.

Joe was a tall, lanky guy, with wheat-colored hair and sky-blue eyes. He looked around at everyone and then raised his hand.

"Let me explain about the last two weeks, okay?" There was immediate silence in the room. All eyes focused on him. "I hadn't taken any time off the whole year I was here," he began, "and I wanted to do some sight-seeing before returning to the States. So, I just took off on a little vacation. I got back yesterday."

Julio interrupted, "Why didn't you say something to us, or Mr. Burke? Nobody knew what happened to you. One minute you were here, the next you were gone. We didn't understand what happened. Besides that, we missed you. So did your students. They kept asking all of us where you were and when you'd be back."

Joe took a deep breath, pondering what to say. He slid his eyes over to the Hindes briefly, then back to Julio. "Yes, I admit it was sudden, but I just had to get away from Burke and that business with – I just had to get away." Again he slid his eyes toward the Hindes. Tom spread his hands but said nothing. "I fly back to the States on Monday," Joe added. "If Sandy, here, decides she'll rent my apartment, I'll stop back here early Monday morning to give her my key and say goodbye to everyone. Right now, though, I should take Sandy over to see the apartment."

Before he could stand up, Rosita asked him what business with Mr. Burke he was talking about. Her eyes bore into his, demanding that he explain himself. Joe looked to Tom for help but Tom shook his head to indicate Joe was on his own. The rest of us looked at each other, curious about what "that business with Mr. Burke" meant. Joe stood up then, clearly anxious to leave now, asked quickly if I were ready, and started for the stairs with me trotting at his heels.

As we headed outside, I asked, "How far is it to your apartment?"

"About five blocks, not too far."

"We're walking?"

"The best way," he said, trying to smile at me. I discovered that Joe had long legs, so I almost had to run to keep up with him. Finally, noticing I was lagging behind and huffing and puffing, he slowed down.

"Sorry," he apologized. He waited for me to catch my breath and then started walking again, at my speed.

I said, "That's okay. At least I got my exercise in for the day."

He chuckled for my benefit but a somberness still hung over him like a dark cloud. He'd been fine until he mentioned "Burke and that business," I thought, and he obviously still hadn't shaken it off. I wondered what the Hindes had to do with it, since he turned to them a couple of times. If Tom knew anything, he sure kept it to himself.

After walking a block in silence, he asked, "What do you think of the school so far?"

"Oh, I love it! I really like the staff there and the students are great and so motivated to learn! I inherited your classes, you know, though I realize that it's the start of a new semester and you haven't met them. What a great bunch of people! Everyone at the school has been so nice and helpful to me. Of course, I've only been here ten days, but so far so good."

"Good people, all of them," he commented. "Rosita's really a dream. Without her, I don't think Burke would be able to run the school. She keeps it running smoothly. By the way, have you met Archie yet?"

"Yes. Interesting fellow."

"Very interesting. Different – in outlook, that is. He'd run the school as a social outreach to the community, if he were in Burke's shoes. He's had some very interesting programs for the school, which the community came to and enjoyed. Burke wasn't interested at first. He couldn't imagine anyone being interested in what Archie suggested, but we've had great discussions, even debates, as well as music and skits and other types of entertainment, all well received. Great guy, but he is also a womanizer, so he'll probably make a pass at you."

"Really?"

'Yup. He's wooed Rosita and Leona and probably would have done the same with Jill, except she's happily married and not interested." That made me wonder if Julio had wooed Rosita, Leona and Jill. Interesting thought.

Before I knew it, Joe stopped in the middle of a street and announced, "We're here." We paused in front of a building hemmed in by other buildings that all looked the same, kind of non-descript, with most of the once-colorful paint flaking off the outer walls, leaving them in different shades of pastels and grays. The buildings looked old and unkempt. On the curb, across from the door to the apartment building stood two large garbage cans. They were banged up, the garbage spilling out of them. Down the street a way, I noticed a (big!) rat scurrying between two other cans.

"Don't look," said Joe. "Rats are everywhere around here."

"They're so big!" I exclaimed. He gently turned me toward his apartment building and we climbed a couple of steps up to the door. He opened it, explaining as he did that it wasn't locked during the day but it was from 10:00pm until 6:00am. You could get out but you couldn't get back in. There were apartments on the first floor but we climbed the stairs to the second floor. The stairs were squeaky and uneven and the banister chipped and broken in places. Slum housing, I thought to myself.

"My apartment is 2-C," he said as he led the way. It was halfway down the hall on the left. He unlocked it and we entered. My initial reaction to it was that it was just a small, cheap, dingy hotel room, much worse than the single dorm room I had pictured. Apart from the bathroom, it had no amenities at all: no kitchen area with a sink, cupboards, counter, cabinets or drawers. No bedroom, closet or dresser. It was just a small empty room with a curtained-off bathroom!

I saw the cot Joe had mentioned which was at the end of the room under the only window, which, like at the Luggage Shack, had only a lattice-like grate. A light blanket lay over the top of the cot along with a pillow. The small table was to our left and the chair next to it had clearly seen better days. The two-burner hotplate sat at the end of the table along with a small cooking pot and frypan. Next to it sat his place setting for one. Pretty austere!

"I know it's not much," he commented, looking at it through my eyes, "but it's a place to start until you find a better place." If Mr. Burke was so eager for me to get a place of my own, at least this would provide a temporary place for me to stay until I found something better.

"Have you lived here the whole year?" I asked.

"Yeah. I planned to find a better place, too, but I got engrossed in my classes and made several friends and just got busy." He shrugged. "I was hardly here, anyway. Then, in May, I became upset with Burke and wanted to leave and go back to the States. I'd hoped to get out of my contract two weeks early so I could do it. I even told Burke to keep my last paycheck, but he still denied me. So I took off rather than sticking around the school. Anyway, it was way too late to move by then. Plus, I liked my neighbors. They were friendly, they fed me, they even set me up with eligible young women!" He chuckled, remembering. "Some of them were pretty cute, but definitely not all of them! Anyway, I need to get out of here and go home. I can't stand Burke, and. . ." he hesitated and eyed me. Then he just sighed.

"And what?" I asked hesitantly, unsure of how much to probe.

"It's a long story," he commented. "We'll talk about it another time."

"What other time?" I asked more bluntly than I meant to, then continued to blunder on, "This is the only day I'll see you, isn't it? Except for dropping the key off on Monday, which will be very brief since you'll be flying out shortly after that."

"Yeah, you're right," he agreed reluctantly, obviously not sure he wanted to explain. Then he made up his mind, "Tell you what, we'll stop for lunch on the way back and I'll tell you the whole story. How's that?"

"That sounds fine." I smiled at him, with my curiosity already kicking into high gear. It was like a little mystery, and how I loved mysteries!

We turned our attention back to the apartment. "If you want this place, I need to know today, so I can tell the landlord," he said. "There are pegs on the wall over there by that door to hang clothes. That door, by the way, goes to the next apartment, but it's locked from both sides so no one can get through it. The bathroom has a sink, shower and toilet which all work, but there's only cold water available, although the water here isn't really cold. It's more like lukewarm, so it's not too bad. I'm also leaving my indoor trash can. You might want to buy some paper bags for it, to carry the trash down to the outside cans. Take it down in the morning, though, not at night when the rats are out. Let's see, what else? Oh, yeah, there's a laundromat around the corner, about halfway down the block." (That was good to know.)

"I'll take your apartment, Joe. It's not exactly what I hoped for, but I think I've worn out my welcome at the Burkes, at least as far as Mr. Burke is concerned, and I need a place to move into."

"Great! I'll let the landlord know and I'll bring you the key on Monday."

As we locked the apartment door behind us, I noticed several other doors in the hall were slightly open and faces of adults and children were peeking out. When they saw Joe, they came out to greet him warmly, big smiles on their faces. Joe explained to them in Spanish that he was leaving and I, the new teacher at the school, would be renting his apartment.

"Cuál es su nombre?" they asked me as they circled around.

"Mi nombre es Sandy."

They all smiled and said *"Bienvenidos, Sandy! Bienvenidos!"* They kept touching my arms, my hair, my clothes. They were definitely friendly – or maybe a little overly friendly. Joe may have liked all this attention, but I felt a bit smothered. Several hung onto my hands, shaking them continually. Finally, we made our escape and headed for the restaurant.

"Have you been staying with the Burkes since you got here?" he asked on the way. I nodded and he went on, "I did, too. So did the Hindes but I'm not sure about Archie. Lovely house they have." His tone of voice went flat when he said that, and I turned to look at him. "Have you wondered yet why they live in such a magnificent home on the shores of the Caribbean, while we teachers have to find crummy accommodations in town?"

"No," I answered slowly. "I hadn't thought about that. I don't understand. Is there a problem?"

"Burke doesn't make that much more money than we do – some of course, because he's the director – but that home is lavish compared to what we have to live in."

I wasn't sure what to say to that, but his comment started me thinking. Were the Burkes living too high off the hog? If so, why? Or was the question, why not? Maybe they were independently wealthy. What exactly was Joe trying to tell me? He didn't elaborate any further but seemed lost in thought. We walked in silence the rest of the way to the restaurant.

Reaching the *restaurante*, he opened the door for me and informed me that this place had the best *burritos* and *tacos* in the city. We were directed to a table. As soon as we sat down, chips and salsa immediately appeared, then water, and then a waiter to take our orders. Never having eaten South American food before, except for the *bifsteak* and what Lolita cooked for the Burkes, I opted for a beef and cheese *burrito,* and was pleasantly surprised. It was definitely tasty! I also got refried beans and Spanish rice with it.

When Joe shoveled the last bite of his taco into his mouth, swallowed it and drank some water, he sighed and sat back in his chair. Facing me he said, "I've told the Hindes what I'm going to tell you now, but I don't think they believed me or believed that Burke would do something bad." He took a deep breath, then let it out. I waited for him to continue. What he was going to tell me obviously disturbed him a lot.

"Back in the middle of May," he began, "I saw Burke taking money from the safe in his office and pocketing half of it, money that belonged to the school, money that's supposed to be used for advertising and reaching more people to attend the school. Our pay is *dependent* on having an adequate number of students enrolled for classes."

My mouth went into an 'O' shape. I don't know what I expected Joe to tell me, but Mr. Burke taking money from the safe was definitely not it. "Did he see you?" I asked

"No, fortunately. The door to his office had been partly open, so I thought it was okay to go in to talk to him. Before I could announce myself, I noticed him standing over at the safe. I stood there a moment, watching, stunned. I saw him take out a couple of stacks of bills, count them, then put one of the stacks *in his pocket!* I got out of there as fast as I could. I was grateful that no one had taken notice of me standing there."

"Wow." I couldn't think of anything more intelligent to say. Instead, I wanted to rationalize Mr. Burke's behavior away by raising alternative explanations, but putting money in his pocket? How does one explain that away? I tried to think.

"Maybe he was just separating the money and -- ."

"Don't!" said Joe sharply. "Don't try to rationalize what he did. Because when he usually takes money from the safe, he has his financial record book out on his desk, and he duly records the amount of money in the ledger. His door is wide open and everyone can see what he's doing."

"Oh."

"Right."

I frowned and sighed. Joe's concern about Mr. Burke's thievery was palpable. Maybe he really had been stealing money from the school. It was hard to get my head around it. This was definitely out of my league.

"And Tom and Jill are aware of this? What was their reaction?"

"They were skeptical. The only 'evidence' I had was that I saw no new advertising up in store windows or at the schools and churches where he usually put them. There were about a quarter less students who enrolled for classes in March and even fewer seemed to be enrolling for June."

I didn't know what to think or say. Surely, Joe wasn't just mad at Mr. Burke for not granting him an early exit and made the story up! He was so believable, so unsettled by it.

"You don't believe me, do you?" he commented quietly, eyeing me closely.

"I want to believe you, Joe. You seem so concerned. But I've only been here ten days, and most of that time I've spent in the library. Plus, I have no knowledge of March's enrollment compared to June's. Anyway, the Burkes seem to be well-to-do, living in that elegant house. Why would he need the money?"

"I don't know. I haven't been able to put my finger on it." Joe sighed. "I just wanted to warn you that all is not perfect at the school. If you do happen to notice Burke acting strangely, talk to Tom and Jill. Maybe the three of you can figure something out."

Joe paid both of our bills as we left, for which I thanked him. We parted there at the *restaurante* so he could return to his apartment to pack and I could return to the school.

I settled back in the library for a while, but I found it hard to concentrate on what I was doing. My thoughts were stuck on Joe's account of Mr. Burke's suspicious behavior. I decided I needed to talk to Tom and Jill and find out what they thought about Joe's story. I found the two of them a little later and asked if we could talk. We went over to a table in Daisy's Corner, got coffee, then settled down.

"I bet I know what you want to talk about," commented Tom. "Joe told you his story about Burke, right? Seeing him at the safe, pocketing money?"

"Yes."

"He told us too, but we didn't know what to make of it. We weren't there, and who knows for sure if his interpretation of what he saw is accurate?"

"So, you don't really put any stock in it?"

"I really don't know, Sandy. It's true that we've been having less and less students enrolling for our classes. I'll also admit that I looked for our advertising signs where he normally puts them and saw very few. But, honestly, it's just hard to imagine Burke doing something that bad. He's got that beautiful home out in the best part of town, what does he need more money for?"

"That was my question, too."

"Burke's not exactly the warmest human being I've ever known, but I can't call him a thief when I myself didn't see him take that money and put it in his pocket." Tom paused briefly, frowning, then added in a lower voice, "On the other hand, Joe is such a straight guy, very ethical. I can't imagine him making up a story like that."

I nodded. "I felt Joe was telling the truth, to be honest. What he saw really bothered him."

"Yeah, I could sense that, too. However, I'm not sure what to do with the information. Who do we report it to? Where do we go with it? The local *policía*, the U.S. agency funding the school, Burke himself?" He shrugged. "I'm at a loss, Sandy. Jill," he said, turning to his wife, "do you have any thoughts on the matter?"

"Not specifically, but I have noticed the attendance dropping, and that we're having less and less fun and stimulating programs offered each month. In fact, we haven't had any for the last two months. Maybe something is going on. I suggest we keep our eyes and ears open and pay close attention to what Mr. Burke does or doesn't do. However, he's hardly around anymore, always running off to meetings. He used to sit and mingle with the students, now he hardly ever does; nor does he take us out to lunch anymore, just for the fun of it."

We promised each other we would keep alert for any behavior on Mr. Burke's part that caused us to be suspicious and would let each other know about it.

. . .

Joe stopped by the school early the following Monday as promised to give me the key to his apartment. He went around to say his goodbyes to everyone and was gone.

Having the key to my very own apartment for the first time in my life, I wanted to move in and be on my own right away. It was clear Mr. Burke was tiring of me staying in his home. He was either brusquer with me than usual or he ignored me. Helen's attitude was quite different. I sensed she was lonely and enjoyed the company. I thought of asking Mr. Burke to drive me to his home so I could pack right away, but then, I thought, he'd have to wait while I packed and then bring me back to the school. I didn't think I wanted to bother him that much this morning. Anyway, I had the library to work on and my two classes to teach yet today, so I pushed the thought aside.

Of course, I could have packed over the weekend – why hadn't I? Despite wanting to move out of the Burke home, I had such ambivalent feelings about that little dingy apartment that it tamped down my enthusiasm. It was so barren, so unwelcoming. Also, I was afraid of feeling isolated there with no one to talk to. The neighbors all seemed friendly enough, but, well, I wasn't comfortable yet around them. Hopefully, that would change in the coming weeks. Sigh! With effort, I pushed all those thoughts aside and returned to the catalog cards still to be rewritten.

Suddenly, it occurred to me that I had to make arrangements with someone – Julio, Aurelio or Mr. Burke – to get me over to Joe's apartment with my luggage tomorrow morning. Mr. Burke might do it, but I didn't want to ask him. So I sought out Julio and Aurelio.

"I don't know, Sandy," answered Julio to my request. "We're pretty busy tomorrow. "We'll probably be able to get you over there sometime, but I'm not sure when, exactly." I must have looked crestfallen, because Aurelio jumped in to say they *would* get me to my new apartment before my 4:00 class, one way or another. Julio nodded in agreement and I felt much better.

When I got to the Burkes' home that night, I packed everything up. I got to thinking about being a single young woman who had never lived alone before. Until I was nine, I lived with Mom and Nana, then just with Nana when Mom took a job in another town and a year later married Don. They settled in Albany, New York and I went to live with them for a few months. At Christmastime, I went to visit Nana and ended up staying with her from that point until I left for college. There I had roommates. Now, however, I'd be completely on my own, living in a foreign country thousands of miles from family and friends. This adventure no longer felt as exciting as it had appeared last month back in the States. Now it felt lonely and scary. True, I was a grown woman who was supposed to be able to handle a job and the responsibility of acting maturely. But I didn't feel mature at the moment. I didn't feel ready to live on my own. Despite my ambivalent feelings about Joe's apartment, I had committed myself to live there. At this moment, I wasn't sure why. Surely, I wasn't that desperate to leave the comfort of the Burke home, was I? Helen was so friendly and nice to me. But there was no way to get out of leaving now. Everyone knew I was moving into Joe's apartment, especially Mr. Burke who seemed very pleased and satisfied with it. Had I upset him somehow? What should I do? I surveyed my packed suitcases and satchel and sat on my bed dejectedly.

Unexpectedly, God planted a reality check in my mind: *Change your attitude and your perspective about Joe's apartment, starting right now!* I could hear Him clearly and I instinctively understood that this whole Colombian experience could turn into a disaster if I didn't change my negative outlook about Joe's apartment. The only way I knew how to do that was to read my Bible, searching for encouraging words from Jesus.

"Do not let your hearts be troubled; believe in God, believe also in me," I read in John 14:1.

"Rejoice always, pray without ceasing, give thanks in all circumstances; for this is the will of God in Christ Jesus for you," I Thessalonians 5:16-18 admonished me.

"Let us therefore approach the throne of grace with boldness, so that we may receive mercy and find grace to help in time of need," preached the author of Hebrews 4:16.

And finally, in Luke 8:25a, were the words I could feel pierce my heart: *"He said to them, 'Where is your faith'?"*

Where *was* my faith? Didn't I bring it down to Cartagena with me? Surely it was strong enough to deal with Joe's disappointing apartment! And how about giving thanks to God in *all* circumstances? I knew of a man who did thank God in all circumstances. I remember trying to do that but found it very difficult. Maybe if I thanked God for Joe's apartment, it would change my attitude about it.

I hung my head and sat that way for several minutes. Then I asked God for forgiveness for accepting the apartment as a *curse*, and not as a *gift*. *Help me, God, to realize that Joe's apartment is a gift. It will provide shelter just as well as the Burke home had, plus it will free me up from relying on Mr. Burke for transportation to and from school.*

There! I had found two positive things about moving into Joe's apartment. Suddenly, I felt like a weight was lifted from my shoulders. That I could think of something positive about Joe's apartment came as a great surprise. That I could consider it a gift from God even more so.

Smiling to myself, I thanked God again for the gift of the apartment and ended my prayer, saying: *Thank you, Lord, for being in charge of my life and for showing me how to replace my negative thoughts with positive ones!*

Feeling at peace at last, I crawled into bed and slept one last time in the Burkes' beautiful guestroom, letting the whoosh of the waves of the sea lull me to sleep.

. . .

In the morning, I stripped the bed for Lolita and lugged my suitcases and satchel to the front door. After breakfast, as Mr. Burke loaded my things into the trunk of his car, Helen took hold of my hands and told me it had been such a pleasure to have me in their home the past two weeks. She said she really enjoyed getting to know me. Then she gave me a big hug and wished me well at school and in my own apartment.

"I really appreciated your hospitality and generosity, Helen," I told her earnestly. "I enjoyed our times together. Thank you for making me welcome here." We hugged again and I didn't want to let go.

Mr. Burke drove us to the school and moments later Julio and Aurelio came over to me and informed me that they could help me move into Joe's apartment if we did it right then. I was thrilled that they made my move a priority. Aurelio went to get the truck and Julio carried my suitcases back down the stairs while I carried my satchel. Everyone yelled "Good luck!" or "*Buena suerte!*" Then we were off. It only took a few minutes to go those five blocks in the truck. I led them up the stairs to my apartment. My new neighbors came out to see what the ruckus was all about, smiled and greeted us and offered their assistance. Julio thanked them, assuring them none was needed. Inside the apartment, they both looked around in dismay but tried to hide it from me.

"You like it?" asked Aurelio cautiously, eyebrows raised.

I shrugged, trying to stay upbeat and positive. "I'll make it work," I insisted. "Anyway, it's home for now. Eventually, I'll want to look for a little bigger apartment, but for the time being, this is it." Both eyed me with concern, which I did my best to ignore. Then they each gave me a hug and left. As soon as the door closed behind them the place suddenly felt as lonely as I had expected it to be, but I quickly reminded myself that God was in charge and this apartment was His gift to me. Although I *knew* that, my faith and confidence from last night threatened to fade away.

Don't give in to those feelings, said His clear, gentle voice in my mind. Last night, I remembered, God's peace had come to me after I read those challenging and inspiring passages. Dropping to my knees at Joe's cot, I worried that my faith wasn't as strong as I thought it was, that it wasn't strong *enough*. I wondered if this was God testing me. I've been tested before, but this time I wasn't sure I was doing so well. I reminded myself, God had promised to be with me always, even here in this apartment. I needed to trust God's promises more. Tears began to flow, the tears of a penitent. I prayed for forgiveness for my lack of trust. I prayed for a stronger faith. I prayed that God would stay with me. And the blessed Lord heard my cry. He cleansed me of my doubt. He lifted me up spiritually. He filled me with a stronger faith. Hope and peace filled me, as my tears subsided and I felt the calmness of answered prayer raise me up.

Slowly I stood and surveyed the apartment. There were things I could do to make the place look more cheerful, I thought, like paint the walls a bright color and definitely get a decent chair to sit on. I could also buy some practical things like hangers for my clothes, a bigger saucepan and a decent *escoba* to sweep the floor. Too bad my first paycheck was so small. I would have gone right out and bought at least one of those things. Standing there, my heart swelled with new hope and a better outlook. *Lord, thank you for the gift of this apartment. It isn't what I wanted, but it's what I have and I'll make the most of it. Help me make it livable enough that it becomes "home" to me.*

I was okay again. Now it was time to unpack and "set up house." I hung up some clothes on the pegs on the wall, put my personal things in the bathroom, and organized my suitcases so I could get at the rest of my clothes easily. I looked around; that was all I could do at this time.

On my walk to the school, I rejoiced that I was really enjoying teaching my students and putting the library in order. The staff, except Mr. Burke, were friendly and supportive. So, I concluded, I wasn't entirely alone, at least not Monday through Friday. I just had to get through two days by myself on the weekends. I had books at my fingertips to read and I could go into the city and sight-see to my heart's content. In the meantime, as I received full paychecks in the weeks to come, I'd get things for the apartment to spruce it up. Sighing with satisfaction, I brightened and walked with a little more pep in my step.

At the school, I took note of the bright coral-painted walls in the lobby with the eye-catching pictures and decorations hung on them, giving me ideas of what I could do at the apartment. The inviting classrooms and the smiling faces of those who worked here put me further at ease. I inhaled deeply and relaxed even more. I think I literally "sauntered" down to Daisy's Corner to get something to eat, I was feeling so upbeat. Afterwards I worked in the library, then prepared for my classes and taught them. After the students all left, it was time for me to return to the apartment. There wasn't much bounce in my step, I'm afraid, but not because I was depressed about the apartment. I was simply wilted from the intense heat and the long day.

Darkness was settling over the city and I became aware of the people milling about on the street. It occurred to me that it might not be safe walking in this part of town as the sun went down. I began to look more closely at the people around me and felt an immediate uneasiness. They didn't look very savory to me. One man on the other side of the street, slightly behind me, seemed to be watching me and following me. He made me nervous and I picked up my speed. He picked up his speed, too, keeping pace with me and still watching me intently. Uneasiness bloomed into fear. *God, keep me safe! Please don't let him hurt me!*

The sidewalks, being old and uneven, were hard to walk on, even in flat shoes like I wore. I inadvertently got too close to the curb and stumbled. I caught myself right away but the man across the street yelled, *"Cuidado, Señorita!"* Be careful! He started to cross the street towards me and I panicked, thinking of the Luggage Man overpowering me and scared that this man might want to do the same thing. My pulse quickened with fear. I sped up, trying to hurry away from him and get to my apartment. I was running the last two blocks, perspiring heavily. He stopped then. Though he didn't follow me any further, he continued to watch me. He might have been a nice man simply concerned for my welfare, but I wasn't willing to take the chance. The Luggage Man had stirred up old fears in me and a renewed distrust of men and their intentions. At my building, I hurried up the stairs and into my apartment, closing and locking the door. I was breathing heavily and dripping with sweat. Dropping onto the kitchen chair, I waited for my breathing to calm down and my body to cool off. I closed my eyes and breathed in deeply. Feeling ashamed that I might have misjudged the man, I prayed for God to give me discernment to tell the good guys from the bad guys. Gradually, my pulse returned to normal and I calmed down.

I decided to shower and get ready for bed. First, however, I needed to use the toilet. Sitting down on it, I idly looked around the miniature space and eventually my eyes lighted on the top of the curtained doorway. Two large cockroaches were joined together up there, doing you-know-what. I was startled at first, but then I think I became a little irrational. Suddenly it was my "mission" in life to separate them and get them out of my bathroom! I jumped up from the toilet without even flushing it and ran out to get the small dilapidated broom that Joe had left behind. It was in the corner of the apartment by the front door. I grabbed it and returned to the bathroom. The cockroaches were still at it. I tried to get the broom handle between the two critters but they resisted my efforts. Instead, they scurried this way and that way to avoid the broom handle while continuing to remain stuck together as if glued. Eventually, in their frenzy, they climbed higher on the wall in their zig-zag fashion, so that I couldn't reach them anymore, even with the broom handle. I was getting very frustrated (but I imagined they were, too, with me interfering with their act of lovemaking!) Then they squeezed into a crack where the wall met the ceiling and scooted out of sight – still stuck together. I didn't know whether to be relieved or not. If they got out that easily, they could also get back in that easily. Gradually, though, I let the tension inside me go. All I wanted to do was shower and go to bed.

I checked carefully to make sure there were no more cockroaches around in the bathroom. Satisfied I was alone, I showered. The tepid water was actually soothing. As it cooled me off, I let thoughts of the cockroaches, the mosquitos, the missing suitcase, the Luggage Man, and the suspicion about Mr. Burke fade away, tamping them down and giving them all to God. As the water cascaded down my back, I softly sang, *"What a friend we have in Jesus,"* one of my favorite church hymns.

I finally got ready for bed, sat on my cot, got out my Bible and turned to my favorite sections of Psalm 139, which included the following reassuring words:

"O Lord, you have searched me and known me. You know when I sit down and when I rise up; you discern my thoughts from far away. . .Even before a word is on my tongue, O Lord, you know it completely. . .Search me, O God, and know my heart; test me and know my thoughts. See if there is any wicked way in me, and lead me in the way everlasting!"

I really believed what the Psalmist said was true for me as well. God has searched me and in spite of that, He knows and accepts me! Those are beautiful words to me. God has been with me all my life; He is with me here in this apartment in Cartagena. I exhaled slowly, resting in that knowledge, and crawled onto my cot.

I was just dozing off when something fluttered in through the grated window above me and landed on my chest. I jumped up with a shriek and swiped at my chest to get it off me. It was another critter, about the size of one of the cockroaches, but with wings. It flew around the room here, there and everywhere, swooping at me in its frenzy, but as soon as it found the window again it quickly flew out. I think I had stopped breathing while it swooped. I now sucked in a lungful of air to get my pounding heart to calm down. You'd think I'd never been around bugs before! Well, not these big things, that's for sure!

What have I done? I asked myself. Why did I tell Joe I'd take his apartment? Why didn't he mention that cockroaches and flying critters visited him here? Gone was the peace. I was devastated. After changing my attitude about the apartment and acquiring a more cheerful outlook earlier in the day, I now felt gloomy and undone. Tears threatened. Angrily fighting them, I decided right then and there that I would not stay in this apartment any longer. There just wasn't enough room for "them" and me. God may be in this apartment, but I no longer wanted to stay here with Him. I quickly got dressed, grabbed my satchel and key to the school, and ran out of the apartment, down the stairs and outside. I headed for the school and was confident that at least I'd be free of unwelcomed company there and be able to get some sleep.

But, surprise! All I got was more of the same, and not much sleep.

The first thing I discovered when I got to the school was that there were no easy chairs to sit on or recline in, which for some reason I hadn't noticed in all the days I'd been here. Mr. Burke's office had a comfortable looking desk chair, but the door was locked. There were lots and lots of hard wooden chairs around, not one of which looked comfortable enough to sleep on. I walked back to Daisy's Corner, hopeful, but her chairs weren't any different from the chairs up front. Now what?

As I turned around in a circle, surveying my lack of options, I saw Daisy's glass display case with some of her tasty treats still in it. Curiously, it appeared as if everything was moving or changing shapes. What was going on? I went closer to find a reason for what I was seeing and found, to my horror, that all the goodies inside the glass case were covered with roaches, ants and other bugs crawling on them, nibbling on them, and dragging small bits of them away. I vowed then and there I would never eat any of Daisy's baked goods again – unless I saw it come hot out of her oven and placed directly on a clean plate that I was holding! I left Daisy's Corner and returned to the lobby, pulling a couple of chairs together into a makeshift bed. They were very hard and very uncomfortable, but it was still preferable to returning to my apartment. I think. Also, I remembered, I couldn't get back in until 6:00am anyway. I hardly slept all night, but I did doze off toward morning.

When Daisy arrived that morning, I told her about what I had seen in her cookie case, and she chuckled. "They have to eat, too," she said nonchalantly. I just stared at her, unable to believe what I heard. She made the coffee for the day and as it perked, she made some fresh donuts, one of which was for me.

Afterwards, I returned to my apartment (it was after 6:00am now) and just fiddled around. I felt listless from lack of sleep and headed over to the cot to take a nap. Then I remembered the flying thing and promptly moved the cot away from under the window and over by the table. I actually fell asleep quickly and slept for a good two hours.

When I woke up, I sat at the table, read some more Psalms, and prayed for God's presence and strength for the rest of the day. In the quiet of the room, I began to hear little rustling sounds. I looked around, trying to place where the sounds were coming from. They seemed to be coming from my suitcase on the floor across from me. Suddenly I saw a blouse bounce up, as if something were underneath it, lifting it. I stared at it, watching if it would happen again. Another blouse bounced up! I bounced up, too, but couldn't get my feet to move over to the suitcase.

What was inside my suitcase? What if it was a rat or. . .*a snake*? I don't know why I thought it might be a snake except that I was scared of them. I asked myself if a snake could slither up the stairs and into my apartment. Of course it could, I promptly answered myself. It climbed up trees, didn't it? My mind began to fantasize all kinds of scenarios. After all, I'd already encountered a horde of mosquitos, copulating cockroaches and a flying dive bomber, so why not a snake, too? But, what if it was poisonous?? Ever so slowly, because I was ever so fearful, I tip-toed over to the suitcase. Very gingerly, I took hold of one of my blouses and oh so slowly raised it up, not wanting to startle the snake, if that's what it was.

To my astonishment, a little mouse stuck his head up through the sleeve of the blouse I was holding! I dropped the blouse, squealing from surprise, and jumped back. Two more mice heads popped up. I didn't know whether to laugh with relief or cry in terror! As it turned out, I think I scared the mice as much as they scared me, because they suddenly hustled out of the suitcase and over to the locked door to the next apartment.

"You better scat!" I yelled at them, watching them wiggle under the door and disappear. I sat back down on the chair, definitely relieved it hadn't been a snake, but this made *six* unwanted, non-human visitors I'd had within twenty-four hours of living in this apartment! Two cockroaches, one dive-bomber and three mice. *Not acceptable!!*

I looked for something to stuff under the door to prevent the mice from returning and remembered I had brought home *El Universal*, the Cartagena newspaper that Daisy had given me. My plan was to read two or three articles every day to improve my understanding of the local dialect and learn more about the city. I hadn't read it yet and wanted to before I stuffed it under the door. Whether it would keep the mice out, I didn't know, but I hoped it would at least slow them down. I took time to stumble through the two articles I'd chosen, getting the gist of them, but not all the details. Then I carefully stuffed the paper under the door to deter the mice. Now, I noticed, it was getting on for 10 am, time to return to the school.

. . .

On the way there, an emaciated looking woman, holding the hand of a four- or five-year old boy, stopped me and asked for a few *centavos*, cents. She and the boy were hungry; would I please help? It was hard to say no to this poor woman who looked to be in her thirty's or forty's and was obviously caring for her grandson. Both looked sickly and malnourished. The woman also had something wrong with one eye which was oozing yellow pus. I gave her a *peso* and she bowed and thanked me profusely. Then she went her way and I went mine. I felt good that I had had a chance to do a good deed for a poor person in great need in Cartagena. I had to thank God, and did, for placing this opportunity in my path. I could share my faith after all!

Two days after having done my "good deed," Julio let me know that Mr. Burke gave his permission for me to go with them to the *barrios*. "But not this Saturday," he told me. "It's kind of a rough neighborhood. Next Saturday, okay?"

Of course I said, "Okay!"

It was payday again and I looked forward to getting a full check this time – my first full paycheck ever! When I got it, I finally felt like a real grown-up. I went to the *supermercado* and splurged on some clothes hangers and a new broom for my apartment! Next payday, I'd get a new chair for the table.

That weekend, since I wasn't going to a *barrio*, I chose to spend some extra hours at the library and get as much accomplished as I could. By now, I had all the catalog cards pretty much rewritten, except for a couple of indecipherable ones that Rosita and Leona could not figure out, either. The cards were separated into English and Spanish and then subdivided into author and title. I certainly wasn't done yet. But I took a breather, stretched and yawned. I was eager now to start matching the cards with the books.

I decided to do the English books first. Walking over to the bookshelves, I looked for English authors whose last names started with "A". When I had an armful of five books, I set them on the card table. Then I arranged them alphabetically and began matching them up with their author and title cards. Then I collected a few more books and repeated the process. By the time I had all the A's collected and put in order, I was ready for another break. I went down to Daisy's refrigerator and saw she had some kind of fruit drink in there, so I helped myself to a glassful. I'd have to have something more later, but this would do for now.

Back in the library, I studied the books piled on the rickety table and pondered how to proceed. The table wouldn't hold many more books without toppling over, so I had to come up with a better plan. Suddenly I had an idea. If I removed all the Spanish books from the shelves and stacked them on the floor on the other side of the library where they would be shelved, I could free up these shelves more quickly and be able to start shelving the English authors and get them off the table. Invigorated by the fruit drink and my inspiration, I set to work. Taking a few books at a time, the Spanish books began to pile up on the floor on the other side of the room. Then, moving all the rest of the English books to the far end, I ended up with lots of empty shelves to begin placing the English books on.

I sat at my desk to catch my breath. Part of me wanted to begin placing all the "A" authors on the top shelf of the first bookcase. The other part of me wanted to go home. When I noticed that it was just starting to get dusk outside – which reminded me of the man walking behind me the other night – I decided to call it a day and go home. Besides, I was hungry and wanted to eat something. When I got to my apartment, I cooked up some spaghetti for myself. How? I took my small saucepan, filled it with water and brought it to a boil on my hotplate. Then I slowly dropped one or two spaghettis in at a time until each one softened enough to stay down in the water. I added more spaghetti slowly until I had enough for my meal. When it was "al dente" I drained it in the bathroom sink and put it on my plate. For spaghetti sauce I used ketchup. It wasn't exactly the way Mom and Nana made spaghetti, but it was the best I could do under the circumstances.

Sunday, I returned to the library and shelved the "A" authors, then began on the "B's and "C's." Feeling tired and achy from bending and stretching so much, I quit early, but I felt really good about the progress I was making. Monday went slower because my muscles were still complaining, but I did get through the "D's" and started the "E's." My two classes went well that evening plus I had time to visit with Rosita and Leona. They both came into the library to check out my progress and complimented me on what I was trying to accomplish. I didn't see Julio or Aurelio, but the Hindes came over to check on me and Archie stopped by in the afternoon. I felt good that evening as I made my way home and decided I was going to do alright after all here in Cartagena, despite all the mishaps of the first week or so and my attitude toward the apartment, which had improved greatly, thanks to God.

In the apartment, the mice only visited every few days now when they were able to chew through the newspaper (which I replaced as soon as possible after they chewed up the old one). Neither had there been any more mating cockroaches or flying dive bombers.

On Friday, Julio met with me to give me instructions about the trip to the *barrio* tomorrow. "We will leave around 3:30 pm," he told me. "We'll swing by your apartment and pick you up. You won't need to bring anything to eat because we're going to one of the richest *barrios* around. They'll have lots of food and drinks for us. You might bring a sweater, though, in case it gets cool in the evening."

A sweater? Cool? One month in this country and I couldn't imagine ever being cool again! But I dutifully got out a sweater to take with me the next afternoon when they came for me. I made a bet with myself that I wouldn't need it. Surely Julio was just being solicitous. Wasn't he?

. . .

I woke up Saturday morning not feeling so well, kind of feverish and nauseous. I had no idea what was causing it, but I was determined not to let it stop me from going to my first *barrio*. Julio and Aurelio arrived promptly at 3:30 and I was ready for them, sweater and all.

Outside of Cartagena, Julio took a road that headed directly into the jungle. The road was virtually non-existent in places, sometimes just ruts, and anything but straight. Half the time the trees, foliage and creeping vines took over the road or severely limited its space. It was both an exciting and a nerve-wracking ride. The closeness of everything sometimes forced me to sit in the center of the back seat in the truck instead of leaning out the window. Birds sang, large animals thundered their superiority, smaller animals made a ruckus back at them, crawling things and snakes did their thing. I just rode along, taking it all in as the sun, shining through the branches of the trees, speckled us with light and darkness. It was as if someone were flipping a light switch on and off quickly, making it either abruptly bright or abruptly dark. I marveled that Julio could find his way. Off and on, I caught a glimpse of bright yellow-orange flowers among the dense growth.

I asked Julio about the *barrios*, what their purpose was.

"Many, many years ago, back in the 1700's, when people were settling in Cartagena, it was determined that the white people should be assured of housing in certain prime areas of the city. San Sebastian. Santa Catalina and Merced. Non-whites, the mixed races of people and minorities were separated to other areas. And it's been that way ever since, but it's not as rigid as it used to be."

"So the *barrios* that we go to are basically where the poorer people live."

"That's right."

"Oh." I sat back in the seat and mulled over what Julio had said until we arrived at our destination.

The *barrio* looked like a small, neat village. The buildings were painted bright colors and the people approaching us wore colorful dresses and *serapes* were already milling around a building where I guessed we were going to show the films. Clearly, this was a prosperous little town.

It was still light out and we alighted from the truck. Several people invited us over to a table laden with all kinds of pastries, a variety of fruit, and a drink I learned was called *limonada de coco,* coconut lemonade. Very tasty and refreshing! Several men were dressed like businessmen and spoke some English.

One man, who appeared to be the mayor of the *barrio,* approached us and greeted Julio and Aurelio. They introduced me to him and he took the time to explain to me that a foreigner had come to their little community and explored the caves outside of it where, to everyone's surprise, he discovered salt. He bought the caves and the fields around them and started a salt mining business. He hired the townspeople to work the mine and, in the past several years, the townspeople had prospered greatly. It was obvious. Buildings were in good repair. Fresh colorful paint made them look cheerful and well-kept and the people walked with heads held high and smiles on their faces.

"We're not nearly as big as the salt mines near Bogotá," explained the mayor, "but we are very happy. We have built a school for our children and are enlarging our church. The people are satisfied with the progress here." We shook the mayor's hand and told him how happy we were for his and the town's good fortune.

It was now starting to grow dark outside and the women began collecting the trays of food and packing everything up. Julio and Aurelio had already gone into the building and I could hear the generator humming before I reached the door. Inside, a screen was set up and a projector was standing ready for the movies. Several benches had been arranged for folks to sit on. Julio had told me on the way here that they always carried the school's equipment with them each time they went to a *barrio,* because so many didn't have their own. Here, however, though they brought the equipment along, they didn't need it because this little thriving town had its own.

Julio joined Aurelio and me inside the small, squat building and the people began to drift in, too. In no time at all, everyone was ready. As if on cue, there was a sudden hush among the people, including the children, in anticipation. Aurelio started the projector and showed first a cartoon for the many children present, who would be taken back to their homes by older siblings after it was done and probably put to bed. After they left, Aurelio put on a film about democracy which showed various types of governments but pointed out the superiority of a democracy such as we have in the United States. There was no direct reference to communism in the film, but it was certainly implied that other types of governments didn't work as well for the people as democracy did. Finally, they showed an old Hollywood movie, with Spanish subtitles, which everyone seemed to like. It was light and funny so there was much laughter, chuckles and giggles from the people.

Afterwards the men and women stood around us as we got into the truck to leave. The women thrust small parcels into our hands; by the smell, I could tell it was some of their yummy creations.

To my surprise, the air had cooled off enough that I was actually glad Julio had told me to bring a sweater along! I slipped it on and settled into the back seat of the truck. I'd just lost the bet I'd made with myself, but that was okay. At least I was comfortable as we rode through the darkened, cooling jungle back to Cartagena. We were much quieter on the way back than we'd been on the way here. Julio had to watch the road more closely for one thing because the headlights bounced up and down as we hit bumps and dips in the road. Plus, we were all tired.

I thought about these two men, one still telling me he loved me and wanted me to live with him, in spite of him being married. I was sure he just wanted another conquest or to brag that he had an American girlfriend. Aurelio, on the other hand, wore his heart on his sleeve. It was clear he had feelings for me, but, except for looking at me longingly, he wasn't vocal about it. Because I liked both of them, I was determined to keep things lighthearted between us, hoping to prevent hurt feelings and situations we would regret later on. In my mind, they were simply part of my adventure here in Colombia, nothing more. I had no romantic feelings for either of them even though Julio was handsome and charming and Aurelio looked like Superman. I thought of them more as my good friends, or even my brothers, but knew better than to say that to them or I'd really hurt their feelings. So far, I seemed to be pulling it off.

Closing my eyes, I thought of the *barrio* I'd just visited. I hoped all the *barrios* we visited would be as pleasant as this one, although I had been informed that this one was richer and better off than all the others. As I relaxed against the car seat, I became aware of my stomach feeling unsettled and remembered that I had felt nauseous and feverish earlier that morning. I still did, I realized. Frowning, I hoped we would be home soon so I could just go to bed and wake up in the morning feeling better.

Unfortunately, I didn't feel better the next morning. If anything, I felt worse. In fact, I spent most of Sunday moping around the apartment, tidying up, napping, or reading a novel. But, when Monday came around, I got myself ready to go to the school, to be the librarian for half the day and teach the other half. I kept how I felt to myself, plastered a smile on my face and greeted everyone cheerfully. That's what a mature young woman does, isn't it?

When payroll Friday rolled around, Mr. Burke arrived quite late. Everyone murmured and whispered among themselves, wondering what was keeping him. They got edgier as morning became early afternoon and then later afternoon. Classes were about to start and still he hadn't arrived. Then, at 3:25, he finally appeared. The staff lined up for their checks, faces full of questions they didn't dare ask. Neither did Mr. Burke offer any explanation or apology for his lateness. The checks were handed out in complete silence. I quickly stuffed the check into my library desk drawer and hurried into my classroom. On Saturday morning, I went to the *supermercado* and bought a new chair for my table and a large saucepan.

We went to a very poor *barrio* that afternoon, which couldn't offer us food or drink in return for showing the films, but they were profoundly grateful for the chance to feel a part of the wider world in which they lived. It made my heart swell with pride that we were able to lighten up their lives a little bit and didn't have to be paid or rewarded for doing it. At that moment, I was proud to be an American, just like the Hindes. We went to all the *barrios,* expecting nothing in return except a warm welcome and a handshake. If they were able, they provided us a drink and possibly a snack. For us, whatever they offered was enough.

On the way back home from the *barrio*, however, like last week, my joy at going to the *barrios* with the guys was off-set by my awareness of feeling more feverish and nauseous. What was going on? I'd gotten all those shots back home before I left, to prevent me from getting sick. Did they miss one of the diseases?

. . .

The following Saturday, we had a totally different experience in a *barrio*. Everything went wrong, beginning the moment we arrived. We could sense fear and tension in the people right away as they stood around looking lost and unsure. They were hesitant to approach us, which was very unusual, nor did they give us a welcoming handshake.

"Qué pasa?" asked Julio of a man nearby. He shook his head and backed away quickly.

The guys looked at each other. "Should we stay and show the movies?" asked Aurelio.

Julio shrugged, then nodded. "We're here. I'm sure some people will come. Let's do it."

"But there are no children and very few women out," I noted out loud, feeling some anxiety about that. Were they in hiding? If so, why?

Aurelio looked uneasy, too. "Like home," he muttered. I was sure he was flashing back to something that had happened in Italy during the war. Yet he went about setting up the generator, the screen, and the projector, loading a film into it. Did he sense the fear in the people, like he had experienced in Italy?

Meanwhile, Julio had approached a cluster of men and tried to find out what the problem was. The people just shook their heads nervously and walked away. Changing tactics, he asked some others if they wanted to see the movies tonight or not. Most nodded yes, although some gave no reply.

One woman then came forward and took charge. *"Todo el mundo! Siéntese! Ahora mismo!"* Everybody!   Sit down!   Right now! Hesitantly, they all began to comply. Mothers emerged from their homes, herding their children forward and sat them down on the ground. The men and older boys slowly began to follow suit and, within a few minutes, a good number of people were seated and ready. Yet, tension still hung in the air and anxiety was etched on everyone's faces.

Dusk was turning quickly to silken darkness, especially with the jungle so close around the town. Aurelio went ahead and started the first film. Whether by choice or accident, it happened to be about American democracy. People stiffened up, eyeing each other, I noticed, but they watched the film intently.

Shortly into the film, unbeknownst to us, four dark-clad figures slipped over to our truck from the jungle and slashed all four tires! They then slipped away as quietly as they had come. But some people noticed the movement out of the corner of their eyes and began to scream, cry and point. Mothers grabbed their kids and rushed them quickly back to their homes. The men stood up nervously, milling about, confused and fearful, frowns on their foreheads.   They looked at each other for directions, for someone to tell them what to do. No one took up the gauntlet. Eventually, they scattered to their homes and left us alone, standing there in the square with all our equipment.

Julio and I stayed with the equipment while Aurelio went over to our disabled truck to inspect the damage. How were they going to repair or replace four tires on a Saturday night in a small jungle-bound *barrio*?

There was no doubt in our mind now about what the problem was in this *barrio* – the communists were here in their midst and getting aggressive. Somehow the communists seemed to know that we were deliberately introducing films on democracy to the people in the *barrios* to offset the web the communists were spinning around the country. These people were definitely scared. They didn't seem to have anyone able or willing to take charge. They were being intimidated and had no police force or army around; no strength of their own; no means of protecting themselves against the threat. With so many people so poor, many might start to listen to their propaganda and begin to slide in their direction.

That was the over-arching problem for the *barrio*, but our immediate problem had to do with a useless truck, no transportation to get home, no place to spend the night, and no way to protect the valuable equipment we had with us. Julio and Aurelio quietly assessed the situation between themselves as I listened. Julio was saying, "One of us will have to stay with the truck at all times because I don't trust the slashers not to return and do more damage to the truck or even try to steal the equipment. So, while one of us guards the truck, the other one will go over and get the equipment ready to bring back. Then we'll take turns watching the truck and bringing the equipment over."

"Or I could stay with the truck," I suggested, "and the two of you could go pack up the equipment and bring it to the truck."

"Not safe!" said Aurelio immediately, emphatically.

"Be reasonable, Aurelio. They're not going to return right now. They've accomplished what they set out to do – thwart us and scare the people."

"What means 'thwart'?"

"It means they stopped us from showing the film about democracy." He nodded that he understood. He and Julio looked at each other, then shrugged.

"Okay," said Julio reluctantly. "But, Sandy, if you *see* anything, or *hear* anything, or anyone *startles* you, *yell* as loud as you can!!" I promised them I would. They slowly trudged back toward the equipment, packed it all up, and, in three trips, returned with it all and packed it in the truck bed. There had been no more activity from the slashers, but, of course, they could have been watching us to see what we were going to do next.

Then Julio turned to me. "We need to find a place for you to spend a couple of nights because we probably won't be able to get tires until Monday or Tuesday."

"But, where?" I asked

"I don't know, but not here. It's not safe." Both Julio's and Aurelio's foreheads were creased with worry, not just for me, I'm sure, but also because it was also going to be very, very hard to find a gas station or a garage in the middle of the jungle. We stood staring at each other, puzzling over what to do.

A few minutes later we became aware of two men approaching us. A quick inspection told us they were men from the *barrio,* not the slashers. They exuded concern and apprehension for us, as well as themselves. They introduced themselves as Ricardo and Juan Tomás and we shook hands. I barely understood their dialect but I gathered that they had an idea where I could go and stay while the guys got tires for the truck. I heard them say *misioneras,* which I was sure meant female missionaries.

Julio turned to me. "Did you understand what they said?"

"Something about missionaries?"

"Yes. They were telling us about a missionary compound about an hour's ride away from here where they're sure you could stay. They would be willing to drive you over there, explain the situation to the missionaries, and ask for their permission for you to stay there for a few days. Aurelio will ride along so he knows where you'll be. I'll stay behind with the truck and equipment. What do you think?"

"I think I'm worried about you two," I said.

"We'll be fine, Sandy. Your safety is what's important."

I reluctantly nodded to them but was afraid of being separated from them. What if the communists, or those who sympathized with them, came back and did bodily harm to them? What if. . . . .

But Julio was already telling the Tomás brothers that we accepted their idea and the brothers went off to get their car. Julio and Aurelio put their arms around me and assured me that they would be fine and so would I. Right.

Fifteen minutes later, we were on our way. It was a slow, bumpy, nerve-wracking ride through the jungle in the dark on a barely discernable road. The car's headlights did little to illuminate the way, but Ricardo Tomás drove confidently. He knew where he was going. Eventually, we arrived at the missionary compound, which wasn't very large. It consisted of three main buildings and several smaller ones. Señor Tomás picked out the smallest of the three larger buildings, drove directly to it and stopped, but left the motor idling. He told us to stay in the car, why, I wasn't sure. It must have been after 10 pm by now, I thought, and the house was very dark and quiet. Everyone had obviously gone to bed already. Out of the darkness, a couple of dogs slowly appeared and came towards the car, tails wagging tentatively, not sure whether to welcome us or bark furiously. Eventually, a light came on in the house, and two women in nightgowns and robes appeared in the doorway, one turning on the outside light so they could see us.

"*Bienvenidos!*" two female missionaries called simultaneously. "*Bienvenidos!*" And they motioned for us to come to them. Ricardo finally turned off the car and we all got out and headed toward the women. The dogs politely escorted us from the car to the house but didn't enter with us. Inside, the two women turned on some more lights and led us into an old-fashioned but comfortable living room. They invited us to sit.

Ricardo Tomás introduced himself and his brother Juan, then launched into an apology for the lateness of the visit and quickly and angrily told them what the communists had done in their *barrio*. Aurelio jumped in and explained what they'd done to our truck and the need for a safe place for me to stay until they could replace the slashed tires. The two missionaries listened intently, not interrupting once. When Aurelio paused from his recitation, the missionaries were shaking their heads at our sad tale.

Then the taller, younger one stood up. "*Qué quieren ustedes beber?*" What would you like to drink?

The men responded, "*Agua, por favor!*"

"*Herven el agua?*" I asked. Do you boil the water?

"*Si,*" they answered together then hurried to the kitchen and returned not only with water, but some rolls, ham and cheese, and condiments. We dug in hungrily; it had been a long time since lunch. Seeing how hungry we were, they went back to the kitchen and returned with more rolls, half of a roast chicken, and coconut water!

Ricardo Tomás ate the most, but Juan and Aurelio weren't far behind. The ladies looked on with pleasure as we devoured what was probably their week's allotment of food.

I noticed the older lady studying me. She asked in English if I were American.

"Yes," I replied.

"Where are you from?"

"Buffalo, New York.

Before she could go on with further questions, the younger one gently interrupted her, also speaking in English. "First, let me assure you that we are happy to let this young lady stay here with us for as long as it takes for you to get your tires." Aurelio jumped up and pumped her hand, thanking her over and over. He then translated what she'd said to Ricardo and Juan who had stood up, too.

Aurelio gave me a big hug and the missionaries walked the men to the door, waiting until they were settled in the car with the engine started and the lights on before turning out the outside light. Then they returned to the living room where I still sat.

"I think it's time we introduced ourselves," grinned the taller one. "My name is Jolene McCormick and I've been a missionary here for six years now. Before that, I was in Honduras and before that Chile." Jolene struck me as a person with a bubbly personality but who could handle whatever came along and deal with it efficiently. She had an infectious smile that I liked, with very short reddish curly hair that surrounded her face like a halo. She looked to be in her mid-forties. I sensed Jolene was also an empathetic person, someone who could tune into the feelings of others, like pain or grief. I noticed it when she was listening to Aurelio talk. I sensed she was aware of his underlying fear and frustration.

"And my name is Lillie White!" chuckled Lillie. "I'm not sure I'm really 'lily' white, but I do my best. I've been in the mission field for thirty years now." Her hair was nearly all white and it was long, flowing down her back. Lillie was obviously the more matronly of the two but they seemed to be compatible and comfortable with each other.

"What is your name? Tell us something about yourself," said Jolene.

So I told them my name and explained why I was down here in Colombia and what I hoped to do when I returned home next year. We talked and shared stories about our families and hometowns in the States. When we finally wound down, Lillie stood up and smiled at me.

"Come with me, Sandy. I'll show you where you can sleep. We even have some clothes you can borrow while you're here. We keep a closet-full for those in need, so there's always something around." The bedroom she took me to was small but more than adequate, a bit on the sterile side, but definitely better than the cot in my apartment.

"The bathroom is right across the hall," she told me, and got me some night clothes, towels and an outfit for Sunday. "I hope you'll come to our little worship service tomorrow morning. We aren't many, but we sing and worship God and pray for those in need."

"I'd love to," I replied. I hadn't been to a church service since I came down here!

I found the bed more comfortable than I expected. I barely took in the thread-bare easy chair, the small dresser and closet before slipping quickly into night clothes and crawling into bed. Sleep came promptly.

Sunday morning I woke up with a headache, which I chalked up to the tension at the barrio last night. I also realized that the nausea was still present and it felt like my fever was rising. I showered quickly. Over coffee, juice and pancakes in their little kitchen nook, Jolene wanted to know more about what happened last night. So, I explained the best I could and added that we highly suspected the four men were communists or communist sympathizers.

Jolene shook her head. "That's the third incident we've heard about this month. I'm so glad no one was hurt, but I'm sure the people were scared to death."

"They were! They grabbed their kids and rushed out of the area so fast I was afraid they'd trample each other in their haste. Have the communists interfered in this area, too?" I asked.

"No, not so far. And I hope it stays that way."

"Well, I firmly believe that God will protect us if the communists should try to do anything at all here," said Lillie. "I believe God protects us against all evil." Then she stood and started to clear the dishes. End of discussion. "We need to get ready for church."

Jolene and I stood too. Together we helped clear the table. Within twenty minutes, we were on our way to church. I have to say it wasn't the kind of worship service I was used to. It was more free-spirited with glorious singing and shouts of 'Amen!' and 'Halleluiah!' during the sermon. It was amazing and uplifting and I felt blessed to be a part of it this morning. In high school, I'd read a meditative devotional entitled, "*Different Pathways to God*." I learned that no matter what name we use for God, no matter how we choose to worship Him, God is the same God of us all and loves and accepts us all. I believe God is pleased with all His people because no matter how we praise His name, we are worshipping Him with our hearts and souls and trying to do His will as we understand it.

The rest of Sunday was spent quietly, reading the Bible or a novel or listening to Jolene play her Spinet piano. I wondered frequently how Julio and Aurelio were faring. I knew they wouldn't be able to get the tires fixed until Monday or later. I hoped they were able to spend the nights someplace safe and that they were able to get food to eat, especially Julio, who hadn't been here last night to get fed by these wonderful ladies. I hoped Señor Tomás would look out for them and keep them safe. To be honest, I felt guilty that I was in such a protected environment with friendly, caring people while they had to rough it. *Protect them, Father. Keep them safe. Don't let the communists return to harass them further.*

By late Monday afternoon, there had been no word from them and that made me concerned, even though I knew it was likely I wouldn't hear from them for another day or two. I wondered, too, if they even had enough money to buy new or used tires. I wanted to get in touch with them, but although the missionary compound had a phone, I wasn't sure about the little *barrio*. I tried not to imagine all the possible things that could go wrong, so I just kept repeating my prayer that God would protect them, keep them safe from the communists, and help them get replacement tires for the truck. As for me, I prayed for patience, calmness and certainty that the truck would get fixed and the guys would come for me soon.

On Tuesday, Lillie noticed I was listless and quiet, and asked if I was sick.

"I'm not sure, Lillie. I have a bad headache and I feel feverish and nauseous."

"Do you have chills, too?"

"Yes. Sometimes."

"Maybe it's malaria," she suggested.

"But I received a shot for that before coming down here."

She felt my forehead. "Yes, you do have a fever. You should try to see a doctor as soon as you get back to the city. We only have a doctor come here to the compound every three months or so, and he was just here a couple of weeks ago. Some diseases down here are deadly, Sandy, so you want to catch it as quickly as possible."

I nodded. "It's probably nothing serious, but thank you, Lillie."

"In the meantime, have a glass of water. It's been boiled."

It wasn't until Wednesday afternoon that a knock came at the door. I joined Jolene there hoping it would be Julio and Aurelio. To my great relief, there they stood, looking hot and dirty and worn out, but they were here! Jolene immediately invited them in, told them where the bathroom was so they could wash up a bit, then told them to come to the kitchen for some food and drink when they were done. They obeyed her gladly. After washing up, they obediently reported to the kitchen to accept a wonderful hot meal and lots of *limonada de coco*.

While they ate, I went to my bedroom and collected the clothes I'd worn and headed to the washroom. Lillie appeared and said she'd take care of them for me, and added that I should just get myself ready to leave when the men were ready. Such sweet ladies! After the guys had finished eating their fill, we all three gratefully and profusely thanked Lillie and Jolene and left.

On the way home, Julio told me in minute detail of the troubles they had in finding a place even willing to help them. Fear of the communists was widespread in the area, he explained. The people were terrified. Finally, yesterday, they found a man willing to do it, if he could do it very early in the morning while everyone slept. They explained to him that he would have to deliver the tires to where the truck was parked in the neighboring *barrio*, and the man agreed. The guys pooled all their resources together for the tires, which between them wasn't much, so the tires they got were of poor quality but, they assured me, they would get us home. Because of the longer drive from the missionary compound back to Cartagena, we didn't arrive at my apartment until late that night. We were all beat, hot and sweaty. I felt bad for the guys.

"Why don't you both stay home tomorrow?" I suggested, seeing they could hardly keep their eyes open. "Sleep, shower, relax. The school can get along without you for one day, I'm sure."

"*Ay, Sandy,*" sighed Julio. "That would be *grandioso!* But, without Burke's approval, it can't happen. Also, we do not get paid when we don't work. However," he added with a tired grin, " I don't plan to arrive until after lunch. Okay?"

"Okay!" I agreed. Turning to Aurelio, I was about to ask him also, but his eyes were closed and he was leaning heavily against the truck. Julio and I covered our mouths and laughed quietly. After Julio and I woke him up enough to get him in the truck so Julio could drive him home, I waved goodbye and went to my apartment.

. . .

By Friday morning, I could no longer deny that my fever, headache and nausea were much worse. Shrugging it off the best I could, though, I got ready to go to the school.

On the way, I ran into the little grandmother with the bad eye and her grandson again. She approached me and timidly asked for money. Her eye looked worse, her dress was dirty, and the little boy looked sickly. Before I gave any more money to her, I decided I wanted to know more about her situation. I asked her and was surprised that she was willing to tell me. She said her husband had died last year in an accident. She said she was twenty-six! The little boy was her son, age eight! Boy, did I guess their ages and relationship wrong! My heart went out to her, but I explained that I couldn't afford to support myself and her and her son, too. She started to weep. When I asked her about her eye, she explained that it got infected several weeks ago, but she didn't have enough money to see a doctor or get medicine for it. I ended up giving her two *pesos*, but I told her this was the last time.

I felt like I'd done enough for them, although I immediately felt guilty and ashamed for thinking that. We were supposed to love and care for all our neighbors, right? Jesus fed five thousand people (John 6:10-14) and after His resurrection He told Peter, "*feed my sheep*" (John 21:17). And here I was, walking away from two very needy children of God. My heart was heavy with concern for them, but I just wasn't making the kind of money needed to care for three of us. Since I wasn't a miracle worker like Jesus, I prayed for guidance.

At the school, I told Rosita and Leona about the mother and child. They were sympathetic, but they both recommended that I stay away from beggars like her, no matter how believable their story was because, said Rosita, "they're like leeches who will single you out every time they see you. You must become hard-hearted and tell them no or avoid them altogether." I thanked Rosita, but when I turned away I immediately thought of Lillie and Jolene offering food and clothes and acceptance to everyone who came to their door, including me! I was a Christian too, hoping to become a minister – could I do any less?! The story of the Great Judgment (Matthew 25:34-36) occurred to me:

"Then the King will say to those at his right hand, 'Come, you that are blessed by my Father, inherit the kingdom prepared for you from the foundation of the world; for I was hungry and you gave me food, I was thirsty and you gave me something to drink, I was a stranger and you welcomed me, I was naked and you gave me clothing, I was sick and you took care of me, I was in prison and you visited me."

I decided to buy the woman and child a meal the next time I saw them. I would put my faith to work, as I had seen Nana do so many times.

Darkness And Light

Leaving Rosita and Leona, I headed for the library and lost myself in the work there. After lunch, Julio came over to me.

"*Hola, Sandy.*"

"*Hola, Julio. Qué pasa?*" He grinned, his white teeth gleaming, his eyes sparkling. I grinned back at him.

"*Voy a la playa mañana. Quieres conmigo?*" I'm going to the beach tomorrow. Would you like to come with me? "We'd go very early in the morning before the sun gets too hot. I'd like you to come with me."

"Julio!" I exclaimed, exasperated but trying not to show it. "You're married and you know I don't go out with married men!"

He shrugged. "Don't consider it a date, then. Just come with me as a friend. There's a nice little beach I'd like to take you to. We don't even have to stay long. But I was thinking you should get to swim in one of our nice beaches while you're down here at least once."

"Who else will be coming?"

"No one else. Just us." I hesitated. I was afraid if I said yes, it would get around the school that we were dating and I didn't want that.

"I'll be good, I promise. Please say yes." He turned on the charm, making me laugh.

"Okay," I agreed. As he walked away, I thought of my bathing suit folded neatly in my suitcase, waiting patiently for me to take it out and put it on. The idea of swimming in the warm Caribbean waters began to work on me. I was glad I said okay to Julio. I dearly wanted to go swimming!

However, I had no idea what a little early morning sun and a little swim could do to me. I would soon find out!

As the afternoon wore on, all of us became anxious because Mr. Burke was very late again coming in with our checks. As we all waited and chatted about it, I found out that Leona's anxiety was for her mother, who was very ill and needed a certain medication to stay alive. Aurelio's mother, I also learned, needed heart surgery. Their paycheck was vitally important to them. I realized, too, that no one here at the school was working for a sufficient wage. They were living from paycheck to paycheck. As the conversations stalled, everyone turned back and stared at the staircase, praying Mr. Burke would come soon. When he hadn't arrived by 4:00, I left to go teach my class. It wasn't until a few minutes before 5:00 that I heard commotion out in the lobby and knew he had arrived. I could imagine the suppressed anger on everyone's faces, the humility of dependence they felt in needing their checks so badly, the desperation and resentment at having to worry if Mr. Burke would come in with the checks or not. I had made arrangements with Rosita before class to collect my check and put it in my library desk drawer. I'd get it during my break. Tomorrow, I planned on going to the *supermercado* and do some more shopping – if Mr. Burke hadn't docked me for the days I spent at the missionary compound. When I picked up my check later during the break, I saw that he had docked me. I couldn't believe it! I flushed with anger, teared up briefly, then pushed it all aside. Someday, I was sure, Mr. Burke would receive his "reward" for his behavior here on earth. That was in God's hands, so I let go of my anger and prepared myself for my next class.

. . .

Beach day! I woke up feeling worse than the day before. On top of the fever, nausea and headache, I was also starting to have diarrhea. What was going on? Was it the food down here? Had I caught a tropical disease? I didn't want to believe that something serious might be wrong and that I really did need to see a doctor. Surely it would pass in a few days.

I barely felt well enough to go to the beach with Julio, but I had promised him and I hated to break my promises. Gritting my teeth against shivering and cramps, I put on my bathing suit with a sleeveless cloth robe over it and went down and waited for Julio. He arrived promptly at 8:00 am (he was always prompt!) and opened the door of his Jeep for me. It wasn't a new car by any means, but it got us to our destination. We arrived at a pretty little beach near the Caribbean but not exactly in the same area Mr. Burke had taken me on my first day here.

The sun was already shining brightly at 8 in the morning, but it wasn't too hot yet. A little breeze buffered it, keeping the heat down. The sky was an amazing blue, as usual, and I could see some foliage on the way down to the beach, but not much because the sand came almost up to the parking area. The soft warm sand squished between my toes delightfully as we headed down towards the water. It'd been so long since I'd been to a beach! The waves seemed to be slow and gentle, creeping up the beach and receding, endlessly. We found a shady tree to settle under and Julio, who had thoughtfully brought a beach blanket along, spread it out and we settled ourselves on it. He even brought a picnic basket with sandwiches and containers of water in it for us. I wondered if he or his wife made it.

I decided to ask. "Who put the picnic basket together? You, or your wife?"

He grinned his charming grin. "I did."

"But, uh, didn't your wife see you and ask questions?"

"Sure, but don't worry, Sandy. I told her I was going to take the new teacher to the beach because she hadn't been to one yet."

"So, she knows I'm a 'she'?"

"*Si*. But it's okay. I told her you were old and heavy-set and wanted to go to the beach just once while you were down here."

"Old and heavy-set? Thanks a lot!" But I laughed and relaxed.

We lathered up with sunscreen and then raced down to the water and splashed our way into it. It was warm and so delightful, everything I had hoped it would be. Plus, it was shallow enough for a long way out that I didn't fear drowning. If I took my glasses off, I wouldn't be able to tell how far away from the shore I was and I wasn't that good a swimmer. We played and splashed until we were water-logged. My glasses were so wet by that time that they were virtually useless to me, but Julio took my hand and led me up to our blanket when we were done. There, we flopped down and collapsed.

"That was wonderful!" I gushed happily. "Thank you so much for bringing me here!" He beamed with pride. Julio pulled out sandwiches from his basket for us, but my stomach flipped and I had to turn away. I did accept a container of water from him and drank it down. I tried to tell my stomach to settle down, but it wouldn't listen to me. Along with it, my head started to pound, the cramps began to hurt and my fever seemed to spike.

We laid on the blanket and sunbathed for a while since the shadow of the tree had shifted off the blanket. To distract myself from my discomfort, I began to ask Julio all kinds of questions about himself, his wife, his children, his education, how he came to be working at the American Language School, and what he thought of the drug cartels and the communists who were invading his country and trying to take over. He answered all my questions without kidding around, which I appreciated. Since he usually responds flippantly or light-heartedly, he must have felt the questions deserved straight answers.

Then he decided he'd been serious long enough, so he grinned and asked me to talk about myself. So, I did, even about wanting to be a minister and a missionary. Being Catholic, Julio couldn't fully understand how a woman could feel a call to ministry, but he didn't laugh at me or phoo-phoo the idea, for which I was relieved.

Suddenly, I felt like I was burning up and wondered if I had gotten too much sun. I looked down at my arms and legs and gasped. I was bright red - everywhere! "Oh, no!" I cried.

Julio looked at me and reacted immediately. He jumped up, pulling me with him, then lathered me with more sunscreen, grabbed my hand and pulled me toward the water. The water now felt wonderfully cool against my hot skin. I just stood there in it until I started to shiver too much. Teeth chattering, I headed back to the blanket and took Julio's shirt, which I hoped he wouldn't mind, and threw it over my shoulders and back and my beach robe over my legs. The beach was crowded now with adults and children all around us frolicking in the sand or splashing and swimming in the water. They made lots of noise and distracted me some, but not enough. Julio finally joined me on the blanket, unaware of my distress. He pulled out two more containers of water for us and offered me a sandwich again.

"No, thank you, Julio," I murmured regarding the sandwich, but I did take the water.

"No? But you'll like my sandwiches! I make them good!" He thrust one at me, but I had to turn away because I started to retch. Just dry heaves, but nevertheless. . . . .

"Hey!" said a surprised Julio. "What the – ? Are you sick?"

"I think so," I mumbled between retches, which continued for some time. Afterwards, exhausted and stomach hurting, I laid back on the blanket. I was shivering badly again and Julio promptly covered me with his shirt and my robe. Frowning and anxious with concern, he hovered over me like a mother hen, brushing my damp hair off my forehead, gently dabbing my face, arms, and the tops of my legs with a wet rag.

"Do you want to go home?"

"Yes," I told him regretfully. "I think I do. I'm so sorry, Julio!" Tears of frustration burned behind my eyes but I fought them. "The beach was wonderful," I told him, "the water was perfect, and you were so kind to think of me and bring me here to swim. But I better go home. I don't feel well."

"*Si, si,*" responded Julio. *"Cómo no!"* Of course! I rolled off the blanket and stood, letting him pull everything together and stuff it in the basket. Then he took my hand and we walked slowly up the beach to where he'd parked his car. In the car, he eyed me carefully, shaking his head. "That's going to be a very bad burn. I'm so sorry, Sandy! I thought coming here at 8:00 in the morning would prevent that from happening. We even used sunscreen."

"I know. It's okay, Julio, it's not your fault. Your plan was perfect, but, I guess I burn easily –more easily than I realized. I'm just not used to your tropical sun yet. But we had fun up until the end, right?"

"*Si,* we did, but I'm sorry you got so burnt!"

"Shh, Julio. It'll be alright. What time is it, anyway? How long have we been here?"

"It's almost 10:00, so we've been here nearly two hours. I'll get you home as quickly as I can. Take a cool shower when you get there and put some of that Calamine lotion on. Do you still have some left?"

"Yes." I leaned my head back on the seat and closed my eyes and stayed that way all the way home. At the apartment, he went up with me and made sure I got in alright. But sadness clouded his eyes.

"I'm so sorry, Sandy. I hope you'll be okay. Please drink lots of water and put Calamine on. If there's an aloe plant around, break a piece off and rub it on your burn, too. It takes the sting away and is healing."

"Thank you, Julio." He pecked me softly on the cheek and left.

Eyeing my new, large saucepan, I grabbed it to boil water in. Boy, was I grateful now that I'd bought it the last time I went to the *supermercado!* When the water finally came to a boil I poured it into the glass, the cup, and the small saucepan left behind by Joe. Oh for a refrigerator with a freezer right now, I thought, to put the water in to cool! Oh for some ice cubes! I sat at the table with the glass of water to wait. As soon as it cooled down enough, I drank it greedily. Then I drank the water in the cup. Then I poured the water from the small saucepan into the glass and drank that, too. I poured the rest of the water left in the large pan into the glass and put more water on to boil.

Getting into the shower, I stood under the tepid water for a long time. Still, I felt like I was on fire. Then I started shivering uncontrollably until even my teeth were chattering. I dried off, put my pajamas on and crawled onto my cot with the flimsy blanket pulled loosely over me. Until it got too hot and I had to threw it off. I turned my pillow over and over trying to find a cool spot on it. Nothing seemed to help. I was shivering and burning up at the same time! I couldn't find a comfortable position. Whatever was wrong with me, I knew the sunburn was not the cause, but it was sure making things worse. I prayed for relief. I moaned in agony and prayed for relief, moaned and prayed, moaned and prayed until I dozed off.

I kept water on to boil all day so I would have enough of it to get me through the rest of the day and night. I got back in the shower repeatedly. Nothing seemed to help. At that point, I wished I had never come to Cartagena! Too many unexpected and unpleasant things had happened in the six-weeks I'd been down here, especially the Luggage Man, the communists' attack, this scary fever, and even this sunburn. Each day my faith had to battle to stay on top of everything. I prayed for God to lay His healing hand on me and make me well, to give me stamina, to keep my faith strong.

The rest of the weekend I stayed in bed. I continued to burn, to freeze, to gulp glasses and glasses of water, to shower, to cry, to wish I could go home. I forced some food down me from time to time but couldn't keep it down. I prayed over and over for God to take away this misery. *Where are you, Father? Please come to me! I need You!*

Just then I felt a cool breeze come through my little grated window and there was no doubt in my mind that it was God coming to reassure me. Smiling with relief, I fell asleep.

By Monday afternoon, I could hardly move. I felt weak all over from lack of food, and my skin felt tight from the sunburn. I debated whether to go to the school at all, but I knew my classes would get dumped on Tom and Jill if I weren't there, so I felt like I had to go. I trudged slowly to school, feeling dizzy and unsteady. Fortunately, I didn't meet that poor woman and her son. I didn't think I could be gentle and kind to them today. I settled in the library for a while, trying to draw on energy I didn't have. Rosita came in to say hello and saw my outrageous sunburn.

"*Ay, Sandy!*" she exclaimed. "What happened? Did you go to the beach?"

I nodded. "Very early in the morning, but I still got burned."

She asked me questions about where I went and when and urged me to use the Calamine lotion a lot and the aloe plant. "Also drink lots of water and take cold or lukewarm showers!" she stressed. She fussed some more over me, but finally left. I wandered down to see Daisy. I had to try and eat something; I just felt so weak and light-headed. I bought a warm roll fresh out of the oven and coffee and sat down at one of the tables to munch and drink. Daisy was eyeing me closely, then came over and sat with me.

"That's a serious sunburn, Sandy. Are you okay?"

"No," I told her honestly. For some reason I felt the urge to unburden myself, and Daisy was the right person at the right time. "I feel awful. It's not all from the sunburn, though."

"What else?" she asked quietly.

"I also have a fever that seems to be rising, a bad headache, nausea and vomiting, and now diarrhea. Sometimes I get really bad chills, too."

"Oh, child! I'm so sorry! That doesn't sound good at all. Have you seen a doctor yet?"

"No," I admitted.

"You need to see a doctor, Sandy. Some diseases get serious very quickly and turn deadly. You need to take care of yourself." She gave my hand a squeeze. Her oven timer dinged just then and Daisy went back to her kitchen to check on it.

Back in the library, I listlessly checked titles of books against their cards and my eyes landed on an English language novel with a picture of a young American woman in some African country on the cover. The title had something to do with healing.

Glancing at the book jacket, I learned it was a story about a woman named Grace who had somehow contracted typhoid fever. The story centered on the efforts of three missionary nuns with a reputation for having healing powers to whom Grace had been brought. The nuns prayed constantly and nursed her day and night. They were determined to help her get through this terrible illness. Enter a young American man who was friends with the nuns before Grace had arrived, but now came weekly to visit them because of Grace. Was the man good or evil? What was the connection between him and Grace?

I was looking for a book with some romance, some suspense or some mystery. This one had possibilities. The title certainly caught my attention, since I needed healing, too. I checked the book out. Maybe it would distract me for a few days, at least.

Julio appeared at the door a little while later. "How are you feeling?" he asked me. "You're still very red," he noted.

"It's only been two days, Julio. But, I promise it'll fade in time. It's alright." I tried to smile at him but it hurt my lips. "I'm just going to sit and read a little bit until it's time for my classes."

"Okay. I'll check on you later. Take care of yourself, Sandy."

I read a couple of the opening chapters of the book until it was class time. Somehow, I got through them. In fact, the classes' energy enlivened me. I even got through the rest of the week, but I didn't go out with the guys on Saturday because I still felt so miserable. When they got back and saw me on Monday, they told me there had been no trouble from the communists this time in the *barrio* they went to. Thank goodness!

When I got home, I read, then slept. I had little appetite, subsisting on water and spaghetti, basically. If I were feeling tolerable, I'd stop and get a *bifsteak* at a restaurant, but the fever seemed to be getting worse so I hadn't done that in a number of days. However, on the plus side, the sunburn was now starting to peel.

The book about Grace's healing was an easy read. She was described by the nuns as a golden-haired beauty, sort of ethereal and delicate. They nursed her and prayed many times a day for her. They did everything they could to help bring her temperature down because it was dangerously high. If it lasted too long, I learned, it could cause brain damage or death. The young man who came to visit was named Doug, and he made Tuesday his regular visiting day. The missionaries were gracious to him, as was their nature, but they worried that he would upset their routine with Grace, or bring germs in that she wouldn't be able to fight off, or even try to get too close to her when she needed isolation the most. Gradually, though, Doug's presence became accepted by the nuns. They even began anticipating his visits and had extra food prepared – he always managed to arrive in time for supper, it seemed. The sweet matronly nuns began to relax and enjoy him. He was charming and entertaining, and he always brought news from their hometown. He eventually revealed to the nuns that he had met Grace about a year ago and was thrilled to know she was here at their missionary compound.

Eventually, one evening after dinner, he asked if he could go into Grace's bedroom to sit with her. The nuns immediately balked at the idea, shaking their heads definitely no, at least not yet. After much assurance on Doug's part that he meant Grace no harm, he only wanted to see her, they came to an acceptable compromise. He would be allowed to go in for a few minutes as long as he left the door wide open so they could see or hear if there were any problems. To their surprise, he willingly agreed. In he went, sat in the chair at the side of her bed and simply studied her. The nuns realized that he really meant no harm to Grace, and they began to suspect that he and Grace had had some kind of relationship when they knew each other a year ago.

Each time he went in to sit with Grace, he progressed from simply sitting on the chair watching her, to gently stroking her hand or playing with her fingers or smoothing her hair off her face. Sometimes, he talked quietly to her. Sometimes he simply bowed his head in prayer. Ultimately, not too many weeks later, Grace's fever slowly began to come down. Everyone breathed a sigh of relief. The nuns and Doug offered prayers of thanksgiving and laughed and relaxed, assuming the worst was over. However, her temperature continued to drop, in fact, to plummet to an unsafe level, as was often the case with typhoid fever, according to the book. A plummeting temperature could do damage and kill her, too. Hustling, the nuns now hurried to snuggle warm blankets and hot water bottles around her to keep her body temperature from going any lower, and increased their praying.

The story kept me interested. There was drama, a possible romance, the faith of the nuns, and suspense about whether Grace would survive or not. I wanted there to be a happy ending (I always do!). Towards the end of the book, I sighed with relief as I read that her temperature leveled off and came back up to normal. The danger truly was over. Shortly afterwards, her eyes began to flutter open. Though she had a hard time focusing at first, she finally looked at everyone standing around her bed watching her expectantly. She smiled uncertainly at them.

"Where am I?" she asked in a weak voice. The nuns explained where she was and how she came to be there. "Oh, yes, the fever. I remember it, I think." Her eyes closed and she slept.

The next time she woke, the nuns and Doug were standing around her bed again. Her eyes lingered on each nun, then paused on Doug's. Frowning slightly, she asked, "Do I know you?"

"I hope so," he answered. "We met last year. On a boat ride, actually." She rewarded him with a sweet smile; she remembered. Doug could hardly contain his excitement. The four left the room quietly and again praised God for bringing Grace through her ordeal. The ending of the book was very satisfying to me. As Grace healed, Doug visited her almost daily. The love that had started blooming the year before began to blossom all over again. A happy enough ending for me! I closed the book with contentment.

Good book, I thought to myself, but what an awful disease! Thank goodness I had gotten a shot for typhoid fever before traveling down here, so whatever I had it wasn't typhoid fever.

. . .

July was ticking away. I could tell my fever was getting higher and the diarrhea, headache and nausea worse. I felt drained by all of them. Yet, for some reason, I still didn't go to a doctor. Well, actually, I had a reason: I didn't want anyone at the school to know that I was sick after only a few weeks down here in Colombia. I was hoping it was nothing and I was making a mountain out of a molehill.

So I plodded on as if everything was fine and dandy. I taught my classes, I worked on the library books and I went out to the *barrios* with the guys, but less and less as I felt worse and worse. Each day was a struggle to hide my growing ill-health – except from my poor landlord. The diarrhea was getting out of control and my poor toilet couldn't handle the overload. Each time it plugged up, the landlord had to come to unplug it. He went from good-natured about it to grumpy and grumpier. I was afraid he'd ask me to leave.

I barely ate two meals a day anymore and that was only because I knew I had to. Mostly I wanted to sleep. I showered morning and night to cool off. My clothes, I noticed, were beginning to look baggy and hang limply on me. I assumed the heat and humidity were stretching them out, though I guessed I'd lost a couple of pounds, too. Not having a mirror to see how I looked or a scale to weigh myself, I was unwilling to believe it was all from not eating. For one thing, I didn't feel thinner; I felt bloated and uncomfortable. I used prayer, my Bible, books from the library, my students, anything to stay busy and not dwell on what was happening to me.

Up until this point, I hadn't seen too much of Archie, but he began coming to the school two or three times a week and then every day. For some reason, he seemed to go out of his way to visit me each time. Then he started inviting me to take walks with him, during which he would spout poetry to me, of beauty and gentleness, love and devotion, poetry he made up on the spot. I was enchanted. He also made up songs and sang them softly to me as we'd walk along. He had a beautiful tenor voice and I loved to listen to him sing. Mostly, though, he took photos of me constantly, in various poses, in special places, or with certain scenery in the background. Some were taken without my knowledge, but most he had me pose for. It was very flattering, naturally, but I didn't think I looked pretty enough or felt well enough for Archie to take so many pictures.

He was very pleasant. He was always solicitous, gentle and attentive. He spoke little about himself except for the basic information which I had already gotten from Rosita. On the other hand, he wanted to know all about me. I told him the basics: age, place of birth, my parents, Nana, Phil, and college. He wanted to know the inner me, too, so I told him about my dreams for the future: ordained ministry and serving as a missionary in Honduras. He studied me, assessing that information.

"What about marriage and a family?" he asked.

"If that's God's plan for me, I'm all for it," I answered truthfully, adding, "I would really like that." He nodded but made no other comments.

Archie only stood about a head taller than me. His skin was dark, and he was as graceful as a dancer when he walked. His square glasses always seemed to slip down his nose, making him look like a professor. We'd walk hand in hand, his camera case slung over his other shoulder. During our walks, we'd find little parks or benches in surprising places. Sometimes, we'd just sit for a while and hold hands. He enjoyed touching my unruly hair, trying to pat it into submission (his afro was always neat and trim). He also liked to caress the sides of my face and kiss my fingers. I knew he was flirting with me (making a pass at me, as Joe said he would), maybe trying to seduce me, but it didn't feel offensive or pushy. Occasionally, he'd lean forward and kiss me lightly on the lips.

One night Archie walked me home and I took him up to my apartment to show it to him. Before I had a chance to say a word, he drew me close and kissed me deeply, lingering there. His hands began to caress my neck and back.

Pulling away so we could come up for air, he told me he was falling in love with me! He wanted to love my body, he said, and especially he wanted to photograph me in the nude. His words were spoken softly, caressingly, as his hands slowly moved down my neck and my back, to my lower back. . . . .

Love? Nudity? Photographing my body? *Oh, Lord, how do I stop this?*

"Archie," I murmured, pulling his hands around to the front of me. "Stop a minute. Please." I backed away from him a little bit but still held his hands. He just watched me, barely moving. "Oh, Archie," I whispered, "I can't do that."

"Why?" he asked after a moment.

I could feel tears burning, wanting to spill. "That's not the way I was raised," I explained, trying not to cry. " It would hurt my Nana and Mom too much. Nor is it what I want to do."

He stood silent a long time while I waited for him to say something. Slowly, he began to nod and a softness came into his eyes. Then he cocked his head to one side and a small smile appeared. "I guess I understand. But I still love you, Sandy. I wouldn't do anything to hurt you, you know. If you're really uncomfortable being nude with me, then we won't do that. I'd still like to have walks and talks with you and continue to photograph you – with your clothes on, of course."

I smiled with relief. "Thank you for understanding. I'm really very shy about my body."

"Someday," he commented after a moment, "you'll tell me why." With that, he kissed me softly and left.

I sat down on the chair, thinking about his profession of love and what that meant for him: candid nude shots? Did he only love me for that? I believed there were some feelings in him for me, but I couldn't help thinking it was just a ruse to get me to pose for him in the nude. Not my idea of love at all. Anyway, I thought, looking down at myself, I really couldn't imagine anyone loving me the way I looked and felt these days. Thinner, peeling skin from the sunburn, tired all the time, not to mention the fever and head, stomach and bowel problems.

I realized I was working up to having a pity-party for myself. Tears threatened again, but I pushed them back. I didn't want to cry anymore. Instead, I got up, got into my pajamas, pulled out my Bible, and read one of my favorite passages from the New Testament, where Jesus healed a sick woman:

"Then suddenly a woman who had been suffering from hemorrhages for twelve years came up behind him and touched the fringe of his cloak, for she said to herself, 'If I only touch his cloak, I shall be made well.' Jesus turned, and seeing her he said, 'Take heart, daughter, your faith has made you well.' And instantly the woman was made well." (Matthew 9:20).

Jesus healed that woman. I was sick, too, but not for twelve years like her, of course. Nevertheless, I yearned for Jesus to heal me. If not right away, then to give me strength to persevere until He was ready to heal me. I prayed, *Thank You Father, thank You Jesus, for Your healing powers. Please remember me, one of Your children. Please heal me, if it is Your will. If it isn't Your will, Father, please keep my faith strong and unwavering and stay close to me. Be gracious unto me. Help me bless Your holy name whether I'm ill or well.*

Monday morning, I woke up angry at myself. I've been expecting God to come down and personally heal me, as His Son had healed that woman with the bleeding problem so many years ago! Why haven't I gone to a modern day healer, a doctor? Why have I tolerated this fever and diarrhea without getting medical attention? I've kept putting it off and now it feels like a crisis!

Right then and there, I made up my mind I would find a doctor and get some help for what ails me – maybe even learn the name of my illness! I decided I would talk to Rosita when I arrived at school and have her recommend a good doctor to see. I did my best to hurry and get ready, but I felt clumsy and slow, unable to move gracefully. On the way to the school, I found myself stumbling a lot, my head burning, my vision blurring, my stomach flipping, and the diarrhea constantly threatening. I felt like a drunk wobbling all over the place! Several times I heard people shout, *"Cuidado, Señorita!"* and felt hands reach out to steady me. I don't know how I made it to the school in one piece without falling, but I did, shaking like a leaf. It took a great effort to drag myself up the stairs. Rosita came to the top of the stairs, gasped, then rushed down, catching me before I fell.

"Sandy! Sandy! What is wrong?"

"Sick," I muttered. "Very sick." She guided me up the rest of the stairs and to a chair.

"You shouldn't be here like this! You need to go home and go to bed!"

"Can't. Can't walk." I tried to tell Rosita I needed to see a doctor and for her to suggest one, but I couldn't get the words out. My mind felt too fuzzy and I had no energy to talk. I could hear her and Leona talking in Spanish about how to get me home. I didn't want to go back home. I wanted to see a doctor. But the words wouldn't come.

"You rest, Sandy," said Rosita coming back over to me. "As soon as Julio or Aurelio come in, I'll get one of them to take you home." She laid a cool hand on my forehead and her eyes got big. She whispered, *"Fiebre!"* to Leona. Fever. I already knew I had one but the alarm in Rosita's eyes told me it was a high fever.

"I need a doctor," I managed.

"You rest, Sandy. The guys will be back soon. We'll get you home in no time." Didn't she hear what I said? Wasn't I talking loud enough? I slumped in the chair I was on and promptly fell asleep.

Julio and Aurelio arrived and Rosita quickly explained the situation to them. Aurelio offered to take me home, but I barely remember him picking me up and carrying me down the stairs and out to the truck. I woke briefly when we arrived at the apartment building but blacked out again and was unaware of him carrying me up the stairs and laying me on my cot. I slept the rest of the day and that night.

The next morning, I thought I was feeling some better. I really did. Or maybe it was just my stubbornness; I don't know. At any rate, I was determined to go to the school again and at least teach my classes. Frustratingly, it took an inordinate amount of time to shower and get ready; I felt like I was moving through molasses. When I was finally ready, I set off for the school. Again, things went fuzzy. But the sun was bright and it hurt my eyes and intensified my fever. I stumbled several times again and several hands helped catch me and keep me upright.

Looking up at the stairs was daunting. How was I ever going to climb them? I sank to my knees and started crawling, hoping someone would hear me and come to my rescue. The next thing I knew, Rosita, Leona and Julio were reaching for me, lifted me up and helped me the rest of the way up and settled me on the nearest chair.

"Sandy," Rosita exclaimed, "why did you come to school today? You are too sick. You need to go to the hospital!"

"Rosita – ." I got no further, as a wave of cramps assailed me and I had to rush into the bathroom. Only I stumbled in my effort to get to the bathroom in time and ended up falling into it. Scrambling to my feet, I pulled open the door of the first empty stall, locking it automatically behind me, then hauled my clothes out of the way and plopped down. . .but not quite in the nick of time. Unfortunately. I was barely aware of the mess I was making.

All the voices and noises out in the lobby blurred into one cacophony of sound. My head pounded in concert with it and everything around me was spinning crazily. I let my head droop, my eyes refusing to stay open. I felt consciousness slipping away, blackness closing in. I could hear people calling my name, but as if from a distance. Then I heard banging close to me and my name being called again. It startled me, but not enough to do something about it. I just wanted to be left alone. For some reason, I didn't seem to have a voice to tell them to go away. I couldn't even think of the right words. Then the banging and the sound of my name faded away as blackness overtook me. Bliss.

The next thing I remember, people were doing something to me and jostling me every which way. Blackness again. Then I felt like I was being half-dragged, half-carried down some stairs and laid awkwardly into – a car? Air blew on me, cooling me, before I blacked out again. Next I was aware of more hustling and being carried upstairs. I was vaguely aware of being laid gently on my cot before blacking out again. I don't know how long I was out, but I woke up to see Rosita and Aurelio leaning over me. I tried to sit up.

"No! No!" cried Rosita, pushing me back down. I felt so weak that I didn't even try to fight her.

I looked around. Besides Rosita and Aurelio, I saw Mr. Burke and Julio and many of my neighbors standing in the doorway trying to see what was going on. Concern and worry were etched on each face and everyone was whispering. I couldn't make out what they were saying, wasn't sure I even wanted to know, so I turned away from them all and faced the wall, wanting to go back to blackness and peace. But there was no peace for me yet. A large burley man shouldered his way through the people at the door and came over to stand by my cot. Everyone closed in behind him, their curiosity growing by the minute.

He called himself *El Doctor* and asked me a series of questions in Spanish, but for the life of me, I couldn't understand a word of what he said. Rosita answered his questions the best she could. Then he laid his hand on my forehead and his eyes got big like Rosita's had. He asked if I had a thermometer. Rosita translated for me and I shook my head no. The doctor then turned to the crowd at the door and asked one of them to get one. Several rushed off and returned with their thermometers. He grabbed one and stuck it in my mouth.

"*Dios mío!*" he exclaimed after he took it out. "*Cuarenta y tres!*" My God! Forty point three!

He rattled off what I assumed were instructions about what to do for me. I closed my eyes and left them to it, but I did recognize that my temperature was in Celsius and wondered what it translated into in Fahrenheit.

. . .

I was so uncomfortable I couldn't relax and sleep but I must have because the next thing I became aware of was lying in a hospital bed with a couple of IV drips and an oxygen tube going up my nose. How did I get here? How long have I been here? What day is it? I had no memory of anything after *El Doctor* taking my temperature.

The second surprise was that I was feeling a little bit better, not quite so hot and feverish. The IV's must be bringing down my temperature, I thought, looking at them with appreciation. Eventually I looked around the four-bed ward I was in. There was a small child across from me with her mother (I assumed) sitting next to her, two women in the other two beds, and me. The room was bright from the sunshine streaming in through the windows, but the room was cool. I looked around at the cream-colored walls, the new-looking equipment and thought it must be a fairly new hospital. I settled back down in bed and closed my eyes. I could almost hear waves lapping against a shoreline in the distance, or maybe I just imagined it. Either way, it lulled me back to sleep.

Sometime later, a doctor and nurse came in and woke me up. They smiled at me, the doctor bowing slightly.

"*Buenos días, Señorita,* he said. When he continued to speak to me only in Spanish, I realized my head was still too messed up from the fever to make sense of what he was saying, so I just shook my head.

The mother across the room yelled, "Caca, peepee!" [American slang words for bowel movement and urine].

"*Si,*" agreed the doctor, nodding.

"I don't think I can right now," I mumbled, embarrassed.

"No? Is okay. *Pero, pronto.*" Soon. I nodded okay but I felt like I had excreted everything out of me when I passed out in the school bathroom. The doctor had his nurse administer something into my IV and shortly afterwards I began to grow drowsy again and drifted off.

The next morning, I woke up to the anxious faces of Rosita and Leona peering down at me. I smiled up at them and patted the bed. They sat down on each side of me and each took one of my hands.

"*Dios mío!*" exclaimed Leona. "You so sick!"

"How are you feeling?" asked Rosita.

"Some better."

"Want to know what happened?" asked Rosita.

"About what?" I asked uncertainly.

"About what happened after you fell into the bathroom and passed out."

"I don't know if I do or not."

"Well, let me tell you anyway. When you stumbled and fell, we started to rush over to help you, but the door closed and you made it into a stall. After a long time, when you didn't come out of the bathroom, all of us crowded in there, calling your name to open the door. When you didn't answer us, we were afraid. The guys took the door off the hinges so we could get to you. We were all shocked at what we saw, but we women immediately kicked the guys out. You had thoroughly messed yourself, the toilet and the floor, and you were unconscious. It scared us so badly! I never knew so much could come out of one person!"

Rosita went on to tell me how they had struggled to clean me up. She said they worked as quickly as they could because, even with Jill Hindes in there helping, it was too hard to keep me from falling to the floor in a heap like a rag doll while they cleaned me up, wiped my clothes off the best they could and then wiped everything down. They said they practically had to carry me out of the bathroom then down the stairs and into Mr. Burke's car for the ride back to my apartment. Then it was just as difficult to carry me up the stairs, wrestle me into my apartment and onto the cot. They wanted to change my clothes for me, get me out of my filthy ones but couldn't. So instead they pulled a clean outfit out of my suitcase for me to have when I returned home from the hospital.

"I'm so sorry I caused you so much trouble," I whispered.

"No, no, no! We were glad to help you! We were just afraid of hurting you." I shook my head at their kindness and thoughtfulness.

I asked about the doctor who came to my apartment. Rosita explained that Mr. Burke had called him from the school and asked him to meet us at your apartment.

"What was my temperature?" I asked. I thought it was forty-something, but I wasn't sure anymore.

"*Cuarenta y tres! Muy alto!*" responded Leona.

I repeated it to myself, hoping my foggy mind would remember it until I could find out what that translated to in Fahrenheit.

By the time Rosita and Leona left, I was worn out and went back to sleep. The nurses came in and out, sometimes but not always waking me up, to give me pills, draw my blood, take my blood pressure, take my temperature, change my IV drips – and to remind me to produce some samples for the doctor so they could be tested to determine what was wrong with me.

I slept a lot that day and the next. At some point I was able to give the doctor his samples. I knew it would take a while to get the results, but I was impatient to know. I was also starting to get antsy and restless as the fever gradually came down and the diarrhea lessened. My sunburn was still peeling nicely. Hopefully, I'd see white skin soon. As I started to feel better, however, I became bored. I had nothing to read and nothing to do. I was tired of lazing around in bed, and really tired of the child's mother constantly chattering loudly to anyone who would listen, including me if she saw me awake. I wanted to go home – such as it was – to get back into my routine. I became aware, from hearing the nurses and aides talking, that today was payday. I wondered if everyone at the school got their checks okay. I wondered what mine would be this time.

The next day, all my frustrations came to a head. Did I forget to mention that I tend to be very crabby when I don't feel well? Well, it's true. To express my foul mood, I yanked out the IV's and the oxygen tube from my nose! I threw off the covers and went searching for my clothes – grateful that they would be clean ones – and probably looked something like a very angry child doing it. The child's mother across from me watched wide-eyed, then ran out and told the nurse what I was doing. A few minutes later, the nurse and the doctor entered the room and came directly over to me. He looked around at my various tubes laying on the bed and the floor, then turned and stared at me.

"*Qué pasa?*" he asked, looking very upset and stern.

Instead of cringing, I became bold. "I want to know the results of my tests! I want to go home!"

The nurse translated what I said to the doctor. Using her as his interpreter, he explained that the tests had been sent to the University to be processed, and the results weren't ready yet. He added that I would have to go to the University myself to get the results if I left the hospital before being released by him. And, he added, he wasn't ready to release me yet because I still had a fever and diarrhea, a bad sunburn, and who knows what else? I listened to his recitation and knew it was all true, but I still wanted to go home. I repeated my request more quietly. Much of my anger dissipated as weariness overtook me.

He let out a long sigh, pursed his lips and shook his head. "*Señorita, por favor! No es posible!*" It's not possible!

"*Si, es posible!*" I retorted angrily. "*Hoy!*" Today! Some of my Spanish was coming back to me.

Shaking his head at me and pursing his lips, he turned and left, but the nurse stayed behind. "If you leave today," she told me, "'Against Medical Advice,' the doctor cannot be responsible for you if you have a relapse."

"But I don't even know what's wrong with me! And I *am* feeling some better. I think I'll be alright now. I'll even make a weekly appointment to see the doctor if he wants, but I really need to go home. I thank you for everything you've done, but I want to leave. Today!"

The nurse was thoughtful for a moment, then said, "Look, the tests results should be back in the next couple of days. Why don't you stay until then, find out what's wrong with you, get the medicine you need, and then go home?"

"I have to get out of here!" I whispered to her urgently.

With a sigh of resignation, the nurse nodded her head. "Tomorrow, though, okay? I'd like to get a couple more bottles of fluid into you first so you'll be rehydrated."

I acquiesced. I was getting too tired to argue anymore and the IV fluids sounded reasonable. "Okay. Tomorrow." She set to work putting a new IV in but not the oxygen, straightened up my bed and brought me a fresh hospital gown to wear.

"Nurse?" She paused and looked at me. "Would you let Mr. Burke, at the American Language School, know I'll be leaving tomorrow and ask him if he'd send someone to pick me up?"

"Yes, of course," she said and walked briskly out of the room. The rest of the day took forever to end. I woke up before dawn the next morning and had to wait a couple of hours for breakfast, which I didn't eat much of anyway. I showered, after my IV was disconnected, got dressed in the clean clothes Rosita had sent in with me, then sat on the side of my bed to wait. I had no idea when someone would come for me, so I stretched out on the bed and slept right through lunch. Finally, Aurelio arrived around 1:30 and took me home. He kept asking if I was alright. I assured him over and over that I was. At the apartment, he hovered over me, unwilling to leave. But alone was what I craved.

I took his calloused hands in mine and smiled up at him. "I'm fine, Aurelio. I am fine. Please don't worry about me. I just need to lie down and rest."

"You so sick," he stammered.

"Yes, but not as sick as I was. I'm getting better." I tried to smile more, to look convincing. "Everything is okay," I assured him again. As I slowly eased him toward the door, he suddenly turned and gave me a bear hug, then left. I stood at the door for a moment after he'd gone until I realized how weak I felt. The cot looked inviting. Come rest a while, it coaxed me, and I decided to do just that.

I slept through the rest of the day; it was fully dark outside when I awoke. I put on a light and wondered what to do with myself. I realized I was hungry, so I made some spaghetti and lathered it with ketchup. After eating, I lounged on the cot. I was ready to go back to sleep again. That is, until I heard the familiar scratching in my suitcase on the floor. Checking the adjoining apartment door, I noticed that the mice had managed to gnaw through the paper I'd stuffed under there –when? – a week ago? But the mice didn't faze me this time. Funny how things get put into perspective for you as you move from one little (or big) crisis to another!

Later, I started thinking about my classes and the unfinished work in the library. I also thought of my Nana, who, if she were here with me right now, would have something to say about this situation. I think she'd say something like, "Now, Sandra, young people tend to have the feeling that they're going to live forever. But they're not. Neither are you. You've been very sick and you may or may not make it. I want you to give yourself time to heal. Jesus is with you, Sandra. It's up to Jesus to heal you. I've had to pray for healing for myself, and your mother when she had that diphtheria as a child. Jesus always brought me through. Don't rush back into things right away as if you're 100% better. Take your time. Go slow."

That's my Nana. She always prayed. She always wanted me to have faith and confidence in God, that He would see me through anything. I sat there and reflected on her words, just as I have done many other times. I missed her so much. I wished she were here with me right now. I let a few homesick tears flow, then smiled, feeling a bit rejuvenated. God willing, I would get better. On that reassuring note, I laid back down on my cot and slept peacefully.

Off to the school I went on Monday, feeling more like my old self. I still didn't have much of a spring in my step, but neither was I stumbling and falling. While I was in the hospital, the end of July slipped right past me and it was now August. I'd been in Cartagena for two months. Though the last month had been rough, I figured I was past the worst of my troubles. My health was returning – slowly, mind you, but I was on the mend. I tried to ignore the still present diarrhea and low-grade fever, assuming they would eventually go away entirely.

When I arrived at the school, I was greeted with open arms, warm hugs, and multiple questions about how I felt. It was a wonderful welcome! Everyone was there, even Archie and Mr. Burke. All of us except Mr. Burke headed to Daisy's Corner for coffee and some of her sweet pastries. Everyone wanted to know what had caused the diarrhea and fever. I had to tell them that I didn't know yet because the test results weren't ready and that I'd have to go to the University to get them when they were.

"When will that be?"

"Probably in a few days. They'll call me when they're ready."

They wanted to know what it was like in the hospital, and I told about my little ward of four, plus one talkative mother. I left out that I threw a tantrum and left "Against Medical Advice." They, in turn, caught me up on the events of the past week at the school. The headline event, of course, was me passing out in the bathroom and ending up in the hospital. Friday, they said, was a little tense until Mr. Burke's arrival with their paychecks. Then our group began to break up. They all patted me on the back, smiling and welcoming me back and wishing me better health and returned to their work areas. Archie had listened to the whole conversation, contributing nothing, and left with the others. I wondered what that was about. Tom and Jill stayed behind to talk to me.

"We have your students," said Tom. "You've got a good group there. I was impressed with Roberto, your youngest student, and both of your classes brought fun and laughter with them. I had no idea some of them could speak as much English as they did! You're doing a fantastic job with them, Sandy!"

I gave him a big smile and thanked him. Then I turned and retreated to the library, trying not to feel smug but feeling it anyway. I knew I couldn't take all the credit. The students were doing all the hard work, not me. I was just there to guide and encourage them.

About an hour later, Mr. Burke came into the library to give me my paycheck, which was only half again, due to my hospitalization. I certainly wasn't going to get rich working here! Mr. Burke suggested I finish out this week in the library and wait until next week to teach again. I was both disappointed and relieved: disappointed because that meant a small paycheck again and I'd miss my students, but relieved because I knew I needed time to get stronger and healthier (per Nana's suggestion to "take it slow"). I worried that the students would somehow feel like they were being punished because I was here at the school but not teaching, but I also realized that being with Tom and Jill meant they were getting the best possible education in the English language!

I settled down to work in the library. Not having enough strength yet to shelve books, I sat at my desk and reviewed the catalog cards to make sure they had all the information needed on them and were properly organized. Then I slowly went around the room, dusting and tidying up. I looked over several possible novels I'd like to read. Running out of things to do, I decided to prepare a few more books to be shelved, resting when I needed to. The books were done through the H's but the I's were barely started, so I searched for I authors, sat at my desk and married them up to their cards, shelved the books slowly – I was already wearing out – and sat down again. I managed to get through the J's and K's before it was time to go home.

The next morning, as well as the rest of the week, I chose to arrive at the school around 10:00 instead of 8:00 and work slowly but steadily through the English authors. I worked on the L, M, N and O authors during the week and could have gotten farther, but during *siesta* time, I usually went home for a little nap, getting back in time to work an hour or so before leaving for the day. I hoped that next week I'd have more energy and would be able to get most of the English authors done. Each day, I tried to arrive a little earlier and stay a little longer at the school but just wasn't able to. I wasn't getting my pep back as quickly as I expected to. More than ever, I wanted to get the test results back and find out what was going on with me.

At least, I thought happily, I wasn't feeling spiritually drained! God was by my side; I felt His presence constantly. He had used the doctor and nurses in the hospital to attend to me there. Since I got back from the hospital, I found encouragement and inspirational words speaking to me from the Bible. My prayers felt listened to. A sense of peace, a cooling breeze, the friendships of the staff soothed and comforted me. Favorite hymns came to mind and I hummed them, or even tried to sing them – I'm glad God loves a "joyful noise" because that's as close as I can come to actually singing! Despite how my body felt, the rest of me was doing fine. My spirits stayed high.

. . .

In the meantime, one very bright event occurred. Aurelio and Julio came to see me in the library and surprised me by saying that they had found an apartment for rent that I might be interested in! It was much nicer than Joe's apartment, they told me excitedly. If I wanted to go see it, they could take me right after lunch. I quickly said yes and began to get excited about getting out of Joe's dinky little apartment, which I hadn't been financially able to spruce up like I had hoped, into something a little bigger and nicer. At noon, we grabbed a quick bite to eat, then took off walking to this new place. It was about one and a half blocks further away from the school, and in a slightly different direction. When we got there, I could see it was in a much nicer part of Cartagena. There was a pretty little plaza area there with many potted plants like colorful orchids and passion flowers stationed all around. There were also some palms and flowering trees and even, Julio informed me, pointing it out, the national flower of Colombia.

Houses and small shops lined three sides of the park with a cathedral on the fourth. The apartment the guys took me to was directly across from the cathedral. I was pleased to see colorful paint on all the buildings and people wearing their colorful *serapes*. How well-kept everything looked! Kids were playing in the park and it warmed my heart to hear their laughter and squeals of delight. What a difference from Joe's (well, my) neighborhood and apartment!

We entered the building and a man met us. He took us down the hall a short way to the first apartment on the left and unlocked the double doors. They opened up into a small area into which I could immediately picture a couple of easy chairs and a little coffee table, forming a small living room. Straight ahead and to the left was a larger room with a double wide window. I could picture a dining room table under that window and maybe even a bed against the wall. Unusual combination, but there was no bedroom per se that I could see. Straight across from the window, to the right of the door, was the kitchen – which boasted a sink, counter, cupboards and room for a stove and refrigerator! Yea! I was deliciously happy!

I also noticed that there was an adjoining door to the next apartment, like in Joe's apartment. Seeing me look at that door, the landlord quickly assured me it was locked from both sides and nobody could use it. I nodded but thought to myself, "except mice!" (Now, where did that thought come from?)

The landlord then led us behind the living room, to the left of the dining room, where a bathroom and a small closet were located. The bathroom wasn't much bigger than at Joe's apartment, but it looked in much better shape.

The guys were pleased with the place and looked to see how I felt about it. I was grinning, very pleased indeed. This place was great!

"Yes!" I told them emphatically. "I love it!" Then, the obvious struck me – there was no furniture in the apartment. Not a cot, a dinky table or a chair. Nothing. "Um," I started, not sure how to express myself after being so delighted with the place. But, Aurelio seemed to read my mind.

"You can rent furniture," he said. "Is easy. Many do it." What a novel idea! It sounded good to me and I started imagining what I'd rent and where I'd put it.

Julio interrupted my daydreaming. "Do you want to rent the apartment?" I nodded my head vigorously until my head protested with pain. Julio then turned to the man and started rental negotiations. At least, that's what it sounded like. They came to an agreement and I found out it wouldn't cost me too much more than what I was paying for the old apartment. Amazing!

The man continued talking to Julio while Aurelio and I stood and listened. Julio turned to me and explained that there were many travelers and hikers who made their way through Cartagena on a regular basis. They needed overnight lodging and this apartment building was one of the designated places for them to stay. If I agreed to take in one or two guests at night, a certain amount of money would be deducted from my rent each time I did. Would I be willing to do this? My only expense would be feeding them in the morning before they left.

That was an intriguing idea! *"Si, si, si!"* I told the landlord. That would certainly make life interesting! The landlord nodded, pleased, and passed me the key to my new apartment, thanked us all, and departed.

Next, we walked a couple of blocks to a furniture rental store and made arrangements for the delivery of two living room chairs, a small coffee table, a dinette set with four chairs (since there would be guests), a single bed, a little nightstand, a dresser, a divider to separate my "bedroom" from the dining room, a stove and a refrigerator for the kitchen. I paid for it all from my paycheck and with some of my American Express checks I'd brought from home, using a good portion of them up. The clerk promised it would all be delivered tomorrow morning. There'd be no shopping in the *supermercado* this week, that's for sure. I didn't have much money left over.

But I was deliriously happy. I linked arms with the guys when we got outside and we nearly danced down the street on our way back to the school, laughing and joyous. People stopped to watch us, smiling at our happiness, even clapping. A couple of teenagers started drumming on their bikes, grinning at us from ear to ear.

I wilted as soon as I got back to the school, of course, but I was content. I would have liked to move into my new apartment right away, but I didn't have the strength or stamina for any more activity today.

Instead, I sat around in the library, reading book jackets and making a list of books I wanted to read. Then it was time to head home to nap a while before packing everything up. The next morning, I was ready for Julio and Aurelio before 8:00. I had even packed up my new chair and *escoba* and all of Joe's things. The apartment looked completely bare. There was nothing left to show that Joe or I had lived in the apartment.

Julio and Aurelio arrived, along with Rosita, about 8:15 and insisted on carrying everything down to the truck for me. I locked the door to my apartment for the last time and said goodbye to my neighbors who were milling around and offering little gifts and bags of food. I hugged them all, feeling more emotional than I thought I would. *"Muchas, muchas gracias!"* I called to everyone, pulling gently away from them and heading down the stairs quickly. I dropped the key off with the landlord and off we went to my new home.

We got there before the delivery van, which was our plan. Rosita had brought her broom, a mop and some dust rags and I had my broom. We set about spiffing the place up in preparation for the arrival of the furniture. The kitchen cabinets were wiped down, the bathroom made to shine, the walls all got a once over, the cobwebs all whisked away, the floors swept and mopped. The windowsill and shutters (not grates!) were dusted and flung open to let in the fresh air. When done, everyone collapsed on the floor, catching their breath. After a few minutes, they began to study the apartment. Almost spontaneously, all began to chime in with their ideas about where the furniture should be placed. They all thought the living room and dining room furniture should go in the larger room with the windows and the bed in the area where the double doors were. I explained that I was thinking of putting the bed in the big room with the dining room table and the living room furniture in the smaller room by the doors.

"Why? asked Rosita.

"I don't want my front door to open up into a bedroom," I answered, shrugging.

"Ah." She nodded her understanding. "Then where will you put the bed?"

I explained how I planned to set up an area in the dining room for my bedroom, using a divider to provide privacy. She had a hard time imagining it but we were interrupted anyway at that moment when the van arrived. I directed the men where the furniture was to be placed and was pleased with the care they took doing it. They even set up the stove and refrigerator for me, so I gave them a nice tip for their efforts as they got ready to leave. Now I was almost broke.

Julio, Aurelio and Rosita all looked pleased with the arrangement and happy for me. We all hugged before they went back to the school.

I sat down at my dining room table, the windows directly behind me open to the morning sun, facing the kitchen. I couldn't stop smiling. This was more like it! This apartment was clean and airy, music filtered in from the small plaza outside, and I could hear kids laughing and playing games. It was heavenly. Also, looking at my refrigerator, I was delighted that I could now buy food and keep it cold. I could get spaghetti sauce and quit using ketchup. I could have eggs and salads to eat. I could buy my own meat and not have to stop in a *cocina* to get a *bifsteak*. Things were going to be so much better now; I just knew it! *Thank you, God, for Your bounty!*

I unpacked. Then I put the various single servings where they belonged in the kitchen. I'd have to buy more of everything since I'd be hosting guests from around the world. Soon, everything was as neat as I could make it in the apartment. Closing the shutters to keep out the intensifying heat of the sun, I left to walk back to the school. I was so tired, but I would be okay once I got there.

On the way, I was surprised to encounter the little lady and her son again. We both stopped.

"*Como está?*" I asked her. She shook her head. Her poor eye looked so much worse and she and the child were so dirty and ragged looking. It tore at my heart. The little boy seemed too listless and lethargic. He didn't look well at all.

"*Venga conmigo,*" I told the mother, motioning for her to follow me. I led them to a food vendor on the corner of the street and bought them two bean and cheese *tacos*, which caused their eyes to open wide and then their mouths. Both mother and son woofed the tacos down. The woman cried with gratitude and hugged me, whispering her thanks over and over. For good measure, I bought two more *tacos* for them and then pried their hands loose from me and sent them on their way. I watched them go with a hitch in my throat, glad I had just enough money left over from the move to do it, sad that they were so desperately hungry and destitute. At least I had made an effort to help them get some food this time, as I had promised myself I would.

I continued on to the school, offering a prayer: *Thank You, Father, for showing me that there are opportunities to serve the poor everywhere. Thank You that I have a job and enough money to share. And thank You, again, for my new apartment.*

I finished out the week at school, working only in the library. I would be glad to have my classes back again on Monday. It annoyed me, however, that I still didn't know what was wrong with me and that the University hadn't called yet. Looking down at myself, I saw how much looser my clothes hung on me, and I finally became a little alarmed. I definitely was losing weight. I also seemed to have a lot of chills these days, about as often as I felt the fever, and I couldn't seem to get my appetite back. The on-going diarrhea still hung around, too, though it had lessened a lot. Even the sunburn was still visible in spite of how much I was peeling.

Grumble, grumble! Stop it! I ordered myself. Obediently, I pushed the negative thoughts down. I remembered that God Himself was my Healer, that He was walking beside me, that He had even been carrying me through this ordeal, like in the poem, "Footsteps in the Sand" (Author often mentioned as Anon, but actually, several persons claim authorship of this poem). I remembered Nana whispering to me not too many days ago to be patient. Taking a deep breath, I vowed (again) to do just that. To be patient. To trust God's healing power. To be joyful and grateful just to be alive.

.   .   .

One Saturday evening I was home relaxing and reading a novel when a wonderful serendipity occurred. I had my shutters open for the fresh air and people-noises of laughter and singing and conversation that floated in. I began to hear someone tapping on a car fender, building up a neat rhythm. Then someone else started hitting something that made a different kind of sound but, surprisingly, when joined together they harmonized. Then a third person added a sweet tenor voice to the mix and a fourth came along and added a deep bass voice. I peeked out the window and looked out on this little spontaneous "concert in the plaza."

Others began to converge on the quartet, slapping their thighs, clapping their hands, adding their voices. Small children jumped around to the music and "danced." The original four, who looked to be in their teens, happened to look up toward my window and saw me watching them. They grinned and nodded their heads toward me as they increased their rhythm to include all kinds of improvisations. I was grinning back at them and tapping on the windowsill in time to their beat. This went on for a good forty-five minutes, and everyone in the park was having a good time. Guitarists even came out of a restaurant from around the corner to add their mariachi music to this home-grown concert. When they eventually wound down, I was simply so grateful to have witnessed this spontaneity that I immediately paused to thank God for the gift of music and how it enriched our souls no matter where we were. Then I sat down at the table to write a letter home about it.

Monday finally rolled around and I got my classes back. My students were as curious about my illness as everyone else was. The first part of each class was spent answering their questions and then asking them what they'd learned in the Hindes' classes so I knew where to pick up. They seemed to be glad to be back with me which was gratifying. So we continued on.

By the time I got home that night, I was bushed. Teaching took more out of me than I expected. I quickly showered, read my Bible and prayed, then fell into my nice comfortable bed and went to sleep. In the morning, I read a couple of articles in *El Universal*, read a few pages in the newest novel I had, picked up my apartment in case of visitors, and wrote letters. I said nothing about the on-going mysterious fever to anyone, however. On weekends, I continued to go with the guys to the *barrios*, if I felt well enough. The memory of the incident with the communists began to fade, although occasionally, we did hear of them causing problems in other *barrios*.

Tuesday, I started to have travelers stopping to spend the night with me. I didn't have to be home when they arrived. The landlord let them in. He knew my schedule, so he could tell them when I'd be home. When I met them, I was struck by how robust and healthy they looked. These people were physically fit, obviously used to hiking over rugged terrain their whole lives. They exuded strength and stamina. Boy, did I feel puny next to them! All of them brought their own bedrolls and slept on the floor in the living room. Every morning as I fed them, we talked about their travels around the world and why they had chosen to come to Cartagena. They shared their stories which both amused and inspired me. Also, I found out they all knew more about what was going on here in Colombia than I did!

The first couple were sisters from Germany, taking a year off from their university studies to trek through South America. They were both blond with long braids. They spoke fluent English and passable Spanish. They informed me that travel to Bogotá was restricted by the communists, who had the roads, trains and planes all blocked, preventing anyone from entering or leaving the city. So, they had to change their plans, would avoid the Bogotá area and just enjoy the rest of the country. I marveled that I knew so little about what was going on in Colombia even after reading the newspaper. I told them about the American Language School and how we taught English to anyone interested in learning it and took movies of all kinds out to the *barrios* to help promote democratic ideals and better farming methods. In our own way, we were trying to help the people resist the communists, I said. I spent a wonderful day with these two gals and was glad I had agreed to take in travelers.

The next couple was a husband and wife team, this time from Italy. Their Spanish was okay, their English poor, so our conversations were in Spanish, with the help of their dictionaries. We laughed a lot and strolled around the town seeing the sights. I took them to the American Language School and explained what we did to help the people resist communism. They applauded our efforts.

Following them were a father and son from Australia. Both had been hikers for many years and had gone on many trips to many countries. The father was a good storyteller and related a lot of their adventures to me with humor and insight, while the son chimed in with missing details. They had been on the road now for over a year.

There were other travelers too. Some only stayed for a few hours instead of overnight. They just needed a meal and a rest stop before traveling on. Other couples knew neither Spanish nor English, so we had to communicate by sign language (how could they manage to travel in foreign countries without knowing some of the language?). A couple of young English men came but just as they settled their things in the living room, one of them bent over double with pain and his companion, fearing appendicitis, rushed him to the hospital. I never heard anything more from them, and hoped their problem was resolved and the man was alright.

All these people seemed to have boundless energy, making me feel sluggish and slow. But I wouldn't trade the experience of taking in these travelers for anything. Their experiences, their animation, their joy in learning about other parts of the world and other peoples enriched my soul and brought joy to my life. Plus, whenever I had these guests in my apartment, I slept peacefully, feeling protected and safe.

.   .   .

One morning when I was between visitors, I was sitting at my dining room table reading the newspaper and started to hear scratching noises in the kitchen. No! I thought. It couldn't be! My head snapped up and I found myself looking with disbelief at *five* mice standing there, staring back at me! They looked like a little family with two large mice and three smaller ones. At least mice didn't scare me anymore. These curious little fellows moved very slowly further into the kitchen, watching me watching them. They seemed alert but certainly didn't appear to be afraid of me.

Carefully, and as slowly as they were moving, I inched up from my chair, picking up my newspaper and rolling it up as quietly as I could, then advanced in slow motion toward them. The mice paused, little heads cocked and noses twitching. As my next step came down by the kitchen doorway, the mice suddenly turned as one and scooted back under the door to the other apartment and to safety. I couldn't help but laugh. They were like mischievous kids, playing a game with me. I did as I did before, I stuffed the newspaper into the cracks at the bottom of the door.

Over the days after that, whenever they were able to gnaw their way through the paper, they would enter my kitchen again and again, and we'd play our game. It was hilarious.

FAITH IN ADVERSITY

The University finally called the school on Thursday, August 15th about my test results and Rosita came quickly to the library to get me. I went to the phone to talk to the nurse and set up an appointment for the next day to go and pick up the results. Boy, I could hardly wait to find out what had caused the 40.3 Celsius fever (and find out what that equaled in Fahrenheit) and all my other symptoms. At least, I think I wanted to know.

On several occasions since I'd had the fever, I thought of the book I'd read about Grace's healing, and wondered if I had picked up a tropical disease like she had. I felt confident I was going to be healed like she had been. I may not have nuns to nurse me back to health, but I had faith in God's healing power. I kept trying to assure myself that I did not have typhoid fever; I'd gotten a shot to prevent it. Grace, I reasoned, was sick so long and her fever went so high before it began to come down – and then it plummeted. My fever didn't do that. It did go up somewhat high and I'm now having some chills and shivering I have to admit, but my temperature hasn't plummet dangerously low like hers had. Exhaling, I gave up trying to figure it out. I'd have the answer soon enough tomorrow.

The next morning arrived. Test results day and pay day both. At least this time I should get a full check, unless Mr. Burke docks me for spending last week in the library and not teaching while I was recuperating. I wondered how late he'd be today, given that he'd been late the last two paydays. I didn't expect him to come in before I left to get my test results. So I wouldn't know how much I made until later today, if I made it back to the school in time. Otherwise, it'd be Monday.

I hired a taxi to take me to the University since neither Julio nor Aurelio were able to. I admit I was anxious, as well as shaking with nervousness and chills. To get my mind off how I felt, I looked out the window and tried to pay attention to what was around me. Part of the road we were on disintegrated into a dirt road for a while and was under repair. Later it smoothed out and became paved again and it was smooth sailing. I saw we were heading toward the Caribbean and I remembered hearing waves ebb and flow from not too far away while I was in the hospital. I could see that the University wasn't far from a hospital so I figured that was the hospital where I was taken. I paid off the taxi driver as I exited and made my way into the main entrance of the University. Inside, I gave the receptionist my name and the name of Dr. Chavez whom I was to see. A young nurse came to escort me through the long, winding hallway to Dr. Chavez's office. Smiling, she ushered me inside.

This was it!

Dr. Chavez stood up behind his desk, stretched across it to shake my hand, smiled at me and invited me to sit. His English was nearly perfect. He appeared to be in his late forties with just a touch of gray in his hair. He looked competent and knowledgeable.

"Ms. Cone?" he asked, continuing to smile.

"Yes." He hesitated a moment, so I spoke up before he did. "Do you have my test results? I'd really like to know what they are." The words were out of my mouth before I realized it. True, I didn't feel like chit-chatting or beating around the bush – I'd been waiting too long to get to the crux of the matter – but still, I felt I was being rude.

"I understand you're in a hurry to know what's wrong with you, but I wouldn't be so eager, if I were you, Ms. Cone."

Oh-oh! "Why do you say that?" I asked, pushing down stirrings of fear.

"You have some serious medical problems," he said bluntly.

Suddenly, my mouth went dry. Put like that, I was no longer sure I wanted to know what my conditions were. Dr. Chavez sat down in his chair and pulled up my chart in front of him. He opened it and studied it for a moment, then he looked at me, leaning forward to engage me fully.

"Have you ever heard of paratyphoid fever?" he asked.

"*Para*. . .?" I simply stared at him, my mouth slack. Grace, in the book I'd read, had typhoid fever – what was *para*typhoid fever? Were they similar?

"Is it like typhoid fever?" I asked tentatively.

"It's actually a form of typhoid, somewhat milder, but not much. You've had a serious bout of it. Did the doctor in the hospital put you on any antibiotics?"

"No, I don't think so, but I'm not 100% sure." (I had left too soon, but I didn't want to mention that).

"We will start them immediately, then.

He paused significantly and I waited, my heart pounding. "The second thing you have is amoebic dysentery, Ms. Cone." I'd heard of amoebic dysentery but I knew only that an amoeba was a tiny one-celled parasite that could get into your bowels and wreak havoc. That's exactly what it did in mine, causing the awful diarrhea!

"The third thing you have is an infection in your kidneys – caused by another nasty bacterium. You'll have to stop using salt immediately, beginning today, and I'll order the medication that will clear that up.

"Fourth, you have a stomach infection, again, caused by a bacterium.

"And, finally, you have a vaginal yeast infection. Unfortunately, especially in hot, humid climates like ours with less than adequate sanitation, this is a common infection in women. Since most people don't have hot running water in their homes, they can't get their hands thoroughly clean after going to the bathroom." I thought immediately of all the diarrhea I'd had in recent weeks and how badly I'd messed in the school bathroom when I passed out.

I'm sure I was as white as a sheet as Dr. Chavez finished his recitation of all my troubles. How could I have caught so many illnesses and infections in such a short time? Didn't I have any resistant at all?

"Let me ask you, have you been boiling your water before drinking it?"

Voice quivering , I told him that when I first arrived, I had stayed with the director of the school where I taught. He told me his maid boiled the water so I drank it, but I learned later she had stopped doing that by the time I got there. And I only drank water, not sodas.

"How long were you there in their home?"

"Two weeks." He shook his head and I hurried on to tell him, "Afterwards, when I had my own apartment, I boiled the water. But, starting my first day, at Mr. Burke's home and at the school where I taught, I drank the water."

"When was your first day at the school?"

"June 2nd. A few days later, I discovered that I could get boiled water at the little café at the school, so that's where I got my water from that point on."

"The damage was done by then." He sure didn't mince words! I looked down, feeling foolish for not having taken precautions on the very first day. I'd been warned not to drink the water unless it had been boiled first and I thought I was being careful. But now I wondered if even my first glass of water in the airport had been boiled.

Dr. Chavez paused, eyeing me closely and lowered his voice before saying, "I'm afraid you are still a very sick young lady, Miss Cone. My recommendation to you is to return to the States immediately, because, frankly, I do not see you getting any better if you stay here. It is not healthy for you here. Do you understand? You could die! Go home as soon as you can!"

I was stunned by what he said and I couldn't help myself; I started to cry. I covered my face with my hands and let the tears come. Dr Chavez came around his desk and sat on the edge near me. He patted my shoulder awkwardly and offered me his hanky. In a softer, kinder voice, he assured me, "You will get better once you go home and are under a doctor's care in the States. I will give you enough medicine right now to start the healing process but you must go home." Standing up, he handed me a printed sheet with the list of my illnesses, information about their causes and symptoms, and the medicines needed to cure them.

"Ms. Cone, get your ticket home as soon as possible!" he stated and left the office. I stood up and walked out of his office in a daze. His nurse met me in the hall and handed me several packages of medicine with instructions on how many and how often to take them. She offered to call me a taxi home and I let her.

. . .

On the ride back in the taxi, I pondered all Dr. Chavez had told me, and summed it up in six scary words: *I was sick enough to die!* For some reason – was it God planting the idea? – my mind flashed to the Book of Job in the Old Testament. I remembered that Job was a *"blameless and upright man who feared God and turned away from evil"* (1:8). God was very proud of Job and knew his faith was unshakable. When challenged by Satan, therefore, God allowed Satan to put Job's faith to the test. Satan wasted no time in killing Job's oxen, sheep, and camels, as well as his servants, and then all of his children (1:13-19)! What a devasting loss for Job!

But Job responded by stating, *"The Lord gave, and the Lord has taken away; blessed be the name of the Lord"* (1:21). How strong his faith was!

Then wily Satan challenged God again. This time he wanted to hurt and afflict Job personally. God, so sure of Job's continuing faithfulness, allowed Satan to do as he wished, and Satan caused Job to become covered with *"loathsome sores from the sole of his foot to the crown of his head"* (2:7). His wife cried, *"Do you still persist in your integrity? Curse God and die!"* (2:9).

But Job responded, *"Shall we receive the good at the hand of God, and not receive the bad?"* Job, to Satan's surprise, did not curse God nor *"sin with his lips"* (2:10).

Clearly, my suffering was minuscule compared to Job's. I hadn't lost a fortune in herds of cattle nor hundreds of servants nor all my children. I didn't have a mate who wanted me to curse God and die. Nor was I covered in boils from head to foot. Neither did friends come to see me to convince me God was punishing me because of my sinfulness. That helped me to put things into perspective. Job had literally lost everything of worth to him. I had no concept for what 'losing everything' meant. I still had my faith in God and my family, the two things I valued most in life.

In spite of what Dr. Chavez said, I believed I would get better. I believed in God's healing power and His love for all His children, even me.

I didn't have my Bible with me to check chapter and verse, but I seemed to recall that after all his friends came to convince him he must have sinned to receive so much pain and loss, Job wanted to "take God to court," so to speak, to question Him about why he was suffering so much and to remind God that he, Job, had continued to praise God even in his suffering. So Job prayed with all his might and God, ever-present and ever-listening, heard his prayer and granted him relief. The boils went away, his health returned. As an extra blessing, God also granted him a new family, new servants, and new herds for his fields.

To take God to court. . .not to *beg* for healing but to *reason with God*, to work it out *together*. Job envisioned meeting with God, well prepared with his arguments, and with confidence that God would give heed to him. *"An upright person [man* in older versions of the Bible] *could reason with God"* (23:7). I was sure an upright *woman* could, too! I began to think that if Job could suffer through the awful things that happened to him and still have the presence of mind to reason with God – not blame Him or curse Him – then I certainly should be able to, too!

But back in my apartment, I was so tired from the emotional upheaval of the day – both from the excitement and then the devastation of finding out what was wrong with me – that the inspiration of Job's faith threatened to fade.

This was my reality, I realized, as I sat at my dining room table. I wasn't an old man who lived a long and prosperous life. I was only twenty-two with my whole life ahead of me. Right? Suddenly, it occurred to me that if I had trouble fighting off illnesses here in Colombia, I'd probably have the same trouble in Honduras! Oh no! Not only was I going to have to give up this unique teaching experience in Cartagena immediately and go home, I was also going to have to give up my dream to go into mission work in Honduras after my ordination! What else was I going to have to give up? Everything? Life?

Could I pray like Job: *"The Lord gave and the Lord has taken away, blessed be the name of the Lord"*? At this moment, I wasn't sure. At this moment, I realized that what I needed was the stronger more "comprehensive" faith I was hoping to acquire at Lancaster Seminary. I needed it now! Right this moment! I needed Nana and her wisdom with me. I needed God to reassure me and ease my fear and anxiety.

Slumping in the chair, I rested my head on the table. So tired. The reality was that I wasn't Job and I didn't have his profound faith. Therefore, I began to worry whether God would heal me as completely as He'd healed Job, even if I *"took Him to court"* with all my arguments well-prepared. Closing my eyes, I prayed for full healing anyway because, like Job, I believed I was a beloved child of God. I'd been faithful to God since He first called my name when I was eight years old. I trusted Him then and I would continue to trust Him now. He had healed Job. He would heal me, too. Then, a pleasant peacefulness took over. I went over and stretched out on my bed and fell instantly asleep.

On Saturday morning, I read the story of Job from beginning to end. I wanted to ponder his professions of faith in the goodness of God no matter what, and his own integrity in the midst of all loss, pain and personal suffering. I wanted to understand what it meant to Job to take

God to court, to plead his case before his Judge, face to face; to declare his integrity and righteousness even in his suffering and all his losses; to *"reason with Him,"* believing he would be *"acquitted forever"* (23:7). When Job was done proclaiming his faithfulness, he also acknowledged his sinfulness and declared, *"Therefore, I despise myself, and repent in dust and ashes"* (42:6). The Lord, hearing and seeing Job bearing his soul, accepted Job's prayer and gave Job twice as much as he had before and blessed his latter days (42:10b-12).

I read the story meditatively, searing his statements of faith into my heart, building up my own faith with his strong faith, loving the part where he took God to court, to face Him, to reason with Him, to persuade Him with arguments proclaiming his faithfulness to God in good times and bad. What a profound book it was! I knew I was the better for having read it through again.

Settling in for a long quiet time with God, I felt the peace *"that passes all human understanding"*(Philippians. 4:7) encircle me. My faith was restored; my heart beat with joy.

　　　. . .

Later, determined not to let on how sick I still was but to rely on my faith and trust in God, I cheerfully went out to another *barrio* with the guys. We had a pleasant time. We showed a film on democracy and I was delighted to hear comments like *"Si!"* and *"Me gusta mucho major!"* coming from the crowd.   I like this much better! Communism was not going to sell in this *barrio!* That positive note bolstered my confidence in the Colombian people and lifted my spirits.

Waking up Sunday morning, I still felt the glow of God's peace within me from the weekend. I decided to celebrate by going to the cathedral across the plaza. I quietly slid into a back pew to observe and worship. It was uplifting and although I didn't understand the Latin liturgy or the Spanish hymns, I understood the devout faith of the worshippers, and the peace and joy on their faces.

By Monday morning my euphoria was threatening to fade because I still felt so miserable and it was wearing me down. None of the medicine had really taken effect yet. Each day, it seemed, I had to ask God to renew my faith because it wasn't always as strong in the morning as the night before. During my morning prayers, God faithfully renewed my faith and raised my spirits for the new day.

So this morning, I knelt by my bed, folded my hands, and closed my eyes. I pondered Job's unshakable faith once again. Then I paused, because I remembered that there were many people in the New Testament who had the same kind of faith and integrity that Job had. I thought again of the woman who suffered from bleeding for twelve years. She thought to herself, *"If I only touch his cloak, I'll be made well"* (Matthew 9:20-22). What great faith she had! Jesus turned to her immediately and told her that her faith had made her well.

I remembered the story of the man born blind, who was healed by Jesus, whom the religious officials tried to discredit by claiming he was sinful, a liar, or had a demon. Jesus assured the man his blindness was not from sin, but so that *"God's works might be revealed in him"* (John 9:3). There was also another blind man, Bartimaeus, a beggar, who wanted to ask Jesus to heal him but was denied by the disciples. Finally, he called Jesus' name loudly, and Jesus, hearing him, called him to come forward. The blind man pleaded, *"My teacher, let me see again"* and Jesus healed him right then and there, telling him, as He told so many others, his faith had made him well (Mark 10:46-52). Then there were the ten lepers who begged Jesus for cleansing (Luke 17:11-19). Jesus told them to go to the priest and do what he said, and they ran off to do it. They were all healed along the way. However, only one leper, a non-Jew, returned to give thanks to Jesus Many others approached Jesus as well, imploring him to heal them or their children or servants, and He healed them all.

I felt the euphoria return. The peace of Christ *"that passes all human understanding"* had come to me again and I felt like I had just taken Holy Communion, so close did I feel to the presence of God and His Son, Jesus Christ.

I showered, made myself a piece of toast with peanut butter and jelly, and got ready to go to the school. On the way there I remembered that Friday had been payday and I hadn't been there to get my check. I needed that check to buy an outfit that fit me to wear home. My clothes were all too baggy and faded. I would also have to call the airlines today and get a ticket. With luck, I could get a flight out first thing tomorrow morning, which meant I'd have to pack my things up tonight. Those were the thoughts flitting around in my mind as I arrived at the school.

When I climbed up to the foyer, I could feel the tension in the air. Everyone was standing around, moping, wringing their hands and scowling. I turned to Tom and Jill, who both looked terribly serious. They motioned me over.

"What's up?" I asked, my heart thumping with concern. What now? Tom said. "We have a problem, a serious one. Burke never came to the school on Friday and we never got our paychecks."

"Oh no! Is he coming in today? I need my check!"

"Yeah. We do, too. So do the others, desperately. I don't know if he's coming in or not but he better, or there's going to be a rebellion."

To see Tom, usually calm, cool and collected, that upset unnerved me. I looked around at the others and understood the tension pervading the room. I went around to say hello to everyone and they all told me how worried they were. I knew Leona and Aurelio had sick mothers and probably the others were struggling with issues in their family, too, that I wasn't aware of. Then it popped into my mind that without my paycheck, I might not have enough money to buy my plane ticket home – let alone a new outfit to wear! Oh no! I headed for the library, now as worried as everyone else. Five minutes later Rosita slipped into the library and sat beside me.

"Tell me your test results," she said quietly.

Startled, I realized I had actually forgotten about them for a moment. Sighing, I said, "It's not good, Rosita." Despite my renewed faith, I began to tear up. I still had all of the conditions, after all. The healing hadn't begun yet. Actually, I felt no different from before Dr. Chavez gave me the medicine three days ago. Even though I was convinced God would heal me, at the moment, it felt far away.

With a sigh, I explained to Rosita. "The doctor told me I have five medical issues. First and foremost I have paratyphoid fever. Second is amoebic dysentery. Third, fourth and fifth are infections in my kidneys, my stomach and the last is a yeast infection. Dr. Chavez also told me that if I didn't immediately return to the States, I could die."

"Dios mio! Ay, Sandy, how awful! I understand the infections you have. And I've heard of amoebic dysentery – that caused your diarrhea in the bathroom before you went to the hospital, right?" I nodded. "That leaves the first thing you mentioned."

"Paratyphoid fever. That's a form of typhoid fever – you know what that is?"

"I've heard of it."

"It's a very high fever that can affect your brain and can also kill you. Paratyphoid fever is a milder version of that, but it can be deadly, too. Dr. Chavez stressed that I should return to the States immediately and get under a doctor's care there."

"Immediately?"

"Yes. He said I could die if I stayed here." My voice caught; my throat tightened up. After I got control of myself, I told Rosita that the doctor gave me antibiotics and other medications to take but urged me to buy a plane ticket home immediately and get under the care of a doctor in the States."

"Oh, Sandy! Let me help you get a ticket home right now!"

"I can't, Rosita" I said, flushing with embarrassment. "Not without my paycheck. I don't have enough money left to buy a ticket. I spent almost all I had on rental furniture for my new apartment." It was hard to reveal information about finances to others. That was private information. Nana and I went without, until we had enough money to buy our food and other necessities. Nana wasn't one to accept pity or charity. But here I was, stranded miles away from home in a foreign country that had a hard time understanding that poorness and poverty were a world-wide phenomenon, not just a local one, and that the United States had more poor and impoverished people than they thought.

Besides the rental furniture, I thought of the money I had shelled out recently for plates, utensils, a chair, a broom, the sick little mother and child, and for the taxi ride to and from the University. Now I was up the proverbial creek.

Rosita asked, "Can't your parents buy the ticket for you?"

"Not really. They can't afford it, either," I confessed, wondering if Rosita could understand me.

She did a double-take before saying, "But everyone in America is richer than we are here!"

"Not everyone, Rosita. We have families living on the streets and under bridges, with their babies and children with them. We have homeless shelters and food kitchens for them. They beg through the day to get enough money to feed their children at night so they won't have to cry themselves to sleep."

She looked at me strangely. "I never saw any of that when I lived with my aunt in Arizona," she declared, but then her facial expression abruptly changed. "Yes, I did, as a matter of fact!" she said. "One time in Phoenix, I saw a mother and her little daughter with cups in their hands, going up to different people outside a shopping center begging for money. I saw people dropping coins into the cups. I asked my aunt about it, but she just said not to worry, it was all a lie. People just didn't want to work, she said, so they begged for money instead. I'm sorry, Sandy, I never realized."

"Sometimes that's true, I'm sure, but most of those people really are in dire need and for whatever reason can't get a job or are unable to work. Thank you for sharing that, Rosita. My parents aren't destitute like that mother and child. Both of them work, but, well, they just don't have the extra cash for a plane ticket." I took hold of her hands, "I need to get some money, somehow, Rosita, I need to go home soon! Can you think of any way I can do this? Please?"

Rosita stated to shake her head no but then she brightened when an idea came to her. "There is a special market in this city," she explained, choosing her words carefully, "not the regular market, but a sort of hidden one, where people buy things from the rich and sell them to the poor. I know now that you're not rich, but you are richer than a lot of people living in some parts of our city."

That was true, I knew, thinking about the woman and child whom I was helping from time to time. Nodding my understanding, I asked, "What kinds of things do these people buy?" Her "hidden market" sounded like the black market to me. Not my cup of tea, but did I have a choice at this point?

"Clothes, jewelry, shoes, anything actually," she replied.

"I don't know how to get involved in something like that," I stalled, interested but wary.

"I will contact a woman I know who does this. She is honest and trustworthy. She will take whatever you give her and pay you, then sell your things to the poor." I couldn't imagine poor people being able to pay much for used clothing so I didn't think I'd get much money for whatever I sold. On the other hand, I didn't have many options available to me to get my hands on enough money to buy my ticket home as quickly as the doctor wanted me to.

"Okay, Rosita. I'll try it."

"*Bueno!*" She was up and out the library door then, back to her desk to contact the woman.

Mr. Burke came to the school in the middle of the afternoon. Everyone stood up expectantly, hopefully, and watched while he entered his office. He stopped at the door, turned around and said, "Okay, line up everyone. But be prepared: it's only half a paycheck."

There were gasps and disbelieving looks, some flashes of anger. I closed my eyes against my own disappointment, wondering how I was going to get home now.

Julio entered Mr. Burke's office first, then Aurelio, Archie, Leona, Rosita, me (the Hindes motioned for me to go ahead of them), and finally the Hindes. Nobody ventured far from the office door after they got their check and everyone turned to Tom, as if he were their leader. They implored him with their eyes to say something to Mr. Burke. Taking a big breath, Tom stepped back into the office.

"Sir, why are we only getting half a paycheck?" he asked. "There are people here who really need their full pay."

Mr. Burke wouldn't look him in the eye. He mumbled something, but no one could catch it. We all stood near the door, waiting for him to explain loudly and clearly what was going on, but he said nothing more.

"Mr. Burke," persisted Tom, "please, can you give us an idea of when we'll get the rest of our paychecks?"

Mr. Burke looked up at him then and scowled. "I don't know!" he shouted. "There's just not enough money to go around! Some costs have gone up. Less students are attending. We don't even have money for special monthly programs anymore. Somebody's spending too much money around here!" He ended by banging his fist down on his desk, causing his container of paper clips to bounce, a few even popping out. Then he shooed Tom out of his office and told him to close the door behind him.

We were all shocked, not just because of the half paycheck, but because of Mr. Burke's temper, too. He accused *us* of spending too much money! Was he referring to Julio and Aurelio buying tires for the truck after the communists slashed them? Didn't he realize that that money had come out of their own pockets? I was pretty sure they never even got reimbursed for that. Then I had a sudden thought – what if he meant *me*? I had bought two large packets of 3" x 5" cards for the library. Was that what he was referring to?

All at once, Tom and Jill both met my eyes and Tom jerked his head toward Daisy's Corner. I knew what we were going to talk about.

"Do you remember what Joe told you?" asked Tom as we settled around a table.

"About Mr. Burke? Yes, I do."

"I think we're in a heap of trouble here. I believe Joe now, that Burke *has* been stealing money from the school. He definitely is not using it to increase the number of students coming here, that's for sure!"

"I've been concerned about his growing lack in interest in the school," commented Jill, "as well as the students, even us. He's hardly here anymore, and when he is, he closes his door and seldom comes out and mingles."

I asked, "What can we do? Is there somebody we could contact, like his boss, if he has one?"

We had no time to continue our conversation, as the others had gradually followed us back to Daisy's and wanted to talk.

Leona was crying. In her rapid Spanish, she explained that her mother was very, very ill. With only half a paycheck, she won't be able to buy the medicine her mother desperately needs.

"And my mother needs a heart operation," Aurelio said quietly.

"And my wife is pregnant again," added Julio.

Archie said nothing, but deep concern dominated his features. Discontent and fear permeated the air all around us and, for a moment, no one else said anything.

"And Sandy has to go home as soon as possible because she is very ill and could die!" announced Rosita into the silence. I froze, my own fear shining in my eyes.

Tom's eyes got wide. "What's wrong? I remember you passing out in the bathroom and ending up in the hospital. I also know you went on Friday to get the results of your tests. What did the results show? What's going on?"

I took a deep breath and everyone became still. "Apparently I'm very sick," I told them tremulously . " I've got several diseases and infections that require me to return home and get under the care of a doctor."

"A doctor can't care for you here?" asked Tom, surprised.

I shrugged. "I guess not, but I'm not sure why. The University doctor said if stay here, I could die."

Everyone gasped. I'd been trying so hard not to let on how ill I really was – although fainting in the bathroom and messing myself, the toilet and the floor almost gave me away – so the severity of my health problems came as a big surprise to most of them. Daisy, listening to us, shook her head sadly. Of course, everyone knew about my sunburn; that was hard to hide.

"Exactly what illnesses do you have?" asked Jill quietly.

With a sigh, I listed them. I wanted to explain them dispassionately, but I didn't succeed. After a deep breath, I added, "I need to buy a plane ticket home *today*. But now I can't because I received less than quarter of a paycheck today. Last time, I got only half a paycheck, because I'd been in the hospital." I stopped talking and covered my face. Saying everything out loud, admitting to my body's inability to fight off those five illnesses, seemed to strip me of all my defenses. Tears ran down my face. I felt like a failure.

As I cried with shame and embarrassment, Julio quietly translated what I'd said into Spanish for Leona. Then there was a moment of stunned silence, followed by an avalanche of exclamations of concern for me in Spanish and English. More tears rolled down my cheeks, but this time in gratitude. Many gave me hugs or squeezed my shoulders. I had to keep repeating, "Thank you!" many times. Then I felt God's presence within and around me. God was here, loving me through the love of these good people. I prayed that all of us would be granted relief from the financial predicament we were in.

All of a sudden, Mr. Burke appeared in the doorway. "What's going on?" he demanded. "What are you all doing back here? Why aren't you working? Just because I couldn't pay you a full salary this time doesn't mean you can just stop working!"

Tom stood up and faced him, a determined look on his face. "We just learned from Sandy about some very serious illnesses she has and her need to return to the States immediately to get under a doctor's care. Less than a quarter paycheck this time, and half a paycheck last time don't give her enough money to buy her plane ticket and none of us can help her out because we're all in the same boat."

Everyone turned expectant eyes on Mr. Burke. After a moment he turned to face me and asked, "What kind of illnesses?" So I repeated them for him. He stared at me, but said nothing.

I added quickly. "I need to go home, Mr. Burke, tomorrow. Which means I need to get my ticket today. The doctor said I could die if I stay here any longer." The words hung in the air while everyone waited for

Mr. Burke to respond. I yearned to hear him say he'd help me, that he'd buy my ticket, or even loan me the money – something!

"I can't help you," he replied coldly, stiffly. Then he turned abruptly and headed back to his office, closing the door firmly. All of us were stunned by his unwillingness to help.

"What am I going to do?" I asked. "Call the airlines and make a reservation, anyway? Or put it off until I get my next paycheck?"

Rosita answered, "Today!" Tom and Jill nodded their agreement. Without waiting for my agreement, Rosita started to head back to the phone on her desk but paused, waiting for me to join her. Dr. Chavez had really stressed going home *now*, but how? Without enough money, no airline would just *give* me a ticket. Mom and Nana sure didn't have the money to pay for it. I felt trapped. Yet, in spite of knowing all that, I nodded to Rosita to make the call. She lifted the phone up to dial and I slowly went out to join her.

However, when the ticket agent came on the line, she regretfully informed me that no tickets were available out of Barranquilla for the next *two weeks*! All the American students down here were returning to the States to go back to school, she said, and the seats were all booked. I was shocked speechless. No tickets available? Two weeks from now, it would be September!

"But I have to go home!" I cried to her. "I'm very sick! The doctor here told me I had to leave *now*!"

"I'm sorry, Miss, there's nothing I can do for you. These seats have all been booked for months."

"How am I going to get home?" I wailed, feeling scared and panicky.

The agent paused a moment. "I'll tell you what. If there's a cancellation, I could call you, but you'd have to be ready to fly out that same day. Could you handle that?"

"Yes!" I wasn't sure how, but I would do my best to make it happen.

"I'll also give you a reservation for September 3rd, the first day we have an opening so, if there's no cancellation, you'll at least have that flight to get you home. Will that work for you?"

I groaned inwardly. Two weeks seemed like a lifetime. But I told the agent, "Yes, thank you so much!" After a pause to build up my courage, I asked her how much a ticket from Cartagena, Colombia to

Buffalo, New York, in the U.S. would cost. When I found out the price, I was devastated all over again. There was no way I could get that much money together in time to pay for the ticket! But I took a deep breath and, relying on my confidence and faith in God (like Job did), I asked her to prepare a ticket for me for September 3rd. She did so and asked for my address so she could mail it to me. I gave her the school's address. Then, holding my breath, I asked when I had to pay for the ticket. She said I could pay when I got to the Cartagena airport.

I exhaled with relief. That would give me two weeks' time to sell whatever I could to the lady who would then sell my stuff to the poor, cash the rest of my American Express checks and collect the other half of this paycheck (I hoped) and my last paycheck on August 30th, which I prayed would be a full check. Rosita gave me a hug and told me she'd watch for the envelope with the ticket. I returned to the library.

Later that day, Rosita informed me that Carmen was the name of the woman who would be helping me sell my possessions. Carmen would meet me in the plaza about 9:00 pm tomorrow, wearing a bright red shawl and sitting on one of the park benches.

The next afternoon around 2:00, Aurelio had to go to a hardware store and, being restless, I decided to walk with him. He thought that was *grandioso*. He became animated and talkative and was the happiest I'd ever seen him. After he got what he needed from the hardware store, we stopped by my apartment for a drink of water. Getting ready to return to the school, Aurelio paused, looking like he wanted to say something. I was suddenly aware of the heat in his eyes, the look of desire on his face, and his hands reaching toward me. I stepped back from him, suddenly a little afraid. He was so big and strong! My mind flashed to the Luggage Man and I remembered how quickly he had grabbed me. If Aurelio wanted to do something like that, I wouldn't be able to stop him. I was too weak yet. He saw my reaction and immediately dropped his arms. The light went out of his eyes and he lowered his head in shame.

"Perdóneme! Perdóneme!" he implored me, backing away toward the door. Then he turned abruptly, grabbed the door handle and was out of the apartment before I could respond.

I collapsed on a nearby chair, my heart pounding. I hadn't realized how intense his feelings had become for me, but then I remembered how often I had caught him looking at me. I should have known. Sandy, I scolded myself, you're too caught up in your own problems to pay any attention to other people!

I didn't want to hurt Aurelio in any way, but this was no time for romance. I was winding down my stay in Colombia, already feeling like a short-timer, getting ready to go home. Besides, my feelings for Aurelio were anything but romantic. Yet, his feelings for me obviously were. It made me inordinately sad. I had come down to Colombia for adventure and I guess romance could be called an adventure, or at least be part of one. However, at this point, with barely two weeks left to go, this was just not the time.

In a way, I could say I "loved" Aurelio, along with Julio and Archie, but in a Christian way, even in a sisterly way. I valued their friendship more than anything. I couldn't believe that I could engender such intense and ardent feelings in three different guys at the same time! Was it because I was an American? Or did they just want to use me to get out of Colombia? I prayed for God to help me with these three men, to be more considerate toward them, to understand them, but not to lead them on in any way.

God's Saving Grace

To distract myself from the misunderstanding with Aurelio, I sorted through my clothes for Carmen's visit and picked out the loosest fitting ones that I could no longer wear. I tentatively added a couple of other blouses and slacks I had brought with me but didn't particularly care for; plus a pair of shoes I hadn't worn once down here. Then I held up two bras in my hand, wondering if they could be sold, too.

That evening, before Carmen arrived, I wrote a letter home explaining, at last, what my health was like and that I would be coming home on September 3rd. At 9:00 pm, I wandered down to the plaza and saw Carmen sitting on a nearby park bench. She was about sixty years old, I guessed, maybe older, a small woman. She stood when she saw me approaching her. We were actually about the same height.

"Señorita," she said. *"Soy Carmen."* I am Carmen. We shook hands. She had long gray hair, her eyes were dark, and her face was almost wrinkle-free, but there were crinkle lines around her eyes when she smiled at me. I had been a little apprehensive about this clandestine affair of selling my things on the black market, but Rosita said this was Carmen's way of helping the poor. The woman exuded calmness and dignity so I relinquished some of my apprehension about this endeavor. Rosita had said Carmen was honest and trustworthy and, since I trusted Rosita, I decided to trust Carmen.

She took my arm and suggested, *"Vamos a su apartamento."* Let's go to your apartment. She walked confidently with her head high and I ushered her inside as if she were a queen.

I worried that what I had to sell was inferior or unsellable, but I had already laid everything out for her inspection on the living room chairs and coffee table. Carmen went slowly from one article of clothing to another, inspecting them all methodically, fingering them gently, and then turned to me.

"*Eran buenos. De América?*" They're fine. American?

"*Si, señora.*"

"*Llámame Carmen, por favor.*" Call me Carmen.

"*Gracias, Carmen.*"

She reached under her shawl and pulled out a red velvet money bag. Counting out many *pesos*, she handed me what she felt my clothes were worth. I would take these pesos to the bank when our transactions were completed to convert them into American dollars. Carmen then produced a plastic bag and carefully folded the clothes and placed them in the bag.

"*Hay más?*" Are there anymore?

"*Si. Pero, otra vez.*" Another time.

"*Bien.*"

She stuffed the bag of clothes under her shawl, gave me a happy smile, and I let her out the door. So that's how it was to work, I thought. Pretty efficient and I had my money right away. Every Sunday, Tuesday and Thursday, I parted with other clothes, my makeup, another stretched-out bra, and my bathing suit (no more tropical sunburns for me!). I hadn't brought jewelry down with me to Cartagena so I couldn't offer her anything like that. Nor had I bought any knick-knacks or ornaments for the apartment. Consequently, I was quickly running out of things to sell her.

It was now nearly the end of August. I would be leaving the following week – if I could scrape enough money together in time. Money from selling my possessions was helping, but I felt like I had a long way to go yet. If I could only think of some other way to make money, but nothing came to mind. Unless I wanted to beg. I scratched that thought immediately! Mr. Burke had not paid anyone the rest of our paychecks from the 16th, and the next pay day was in a couple of days. I prayed and prayed to get the other half of the last paycheck, as meager as that would be, and a full check for this pay period. Thankfully, even though not paid for yet, I had my ticket in hand, safely tucked in my Bible.

In the meantime, I continued taking all my medicines and fighting my various illnesses. I knew the fever was slowly coming down but it definitely wasn't gone. The diarrhea was much better as were the other conditions. But, if the doctor was to be believed, I was still not out of the woods. Weary of the problems of the past three months, I couldn't wait to go home. I no longer wanted to be in beautiful Cartagena. The library was pretty much in order at the school and my students again would be split between Tom and Jill. I'd miss everyone, but I felt the urgency of going home outweighed that. What an abbreviated unpleasant, adventurous "year abroad" this was turning out to be!

. . .

My last payday arrived, but Mr. Burke didn't. Everyone was restless and apprehensive, milling around and muttering swear words to themselves. Leona was weeping uncontrollably. Rosita whispered to me that Leona's mother was nearly comatose from the lack of her medication. Julio told us his wife was throwing temper tantrums now because she couldn't afford to go to the doctor and was worried about her unborn child. Aurelio's mother still needed an operation for her heart. What a sad state we were in! Large and small crises had become gigantic ones within a two-week period of time!

By noon, we were all mutinous and ready to drive out to Mr. Burke's home and demand to be paid. Most refused to do any work at the school and we teachers decided to cancel that evening's classes. At 3:00, everyone gathered at the top of the stairs, ready to head down and climb into the truck to go see Mr. Burke, when Mr. Burke suddenly appeared at the foot of the stairs and started up. The people parted for him, but he stopped at the top of the stairs and smiled a lopsided smile at everyone.

"I have your checks," he announced.

"Full checks?" asked Tom boldly.

"Well, almost," he hedged, "at least more than you got the last time." He headed for his office, opening the door and telling everyone to line up. I nudged Leona to go first, since her need was the greatest. Aurelio and Julio went next. Then Rosita and me and the Hindes. Archie wasn't there.

As I opened my envelope, my heart sank. It wasn't even half a paycheck! In dismay, I realized that I wouldn't have enough money to pay for my ticket! What was I going to do now? I'd sold every possible article of clothing I could. I had to keep something to wear home! I heard others around me muttering with dissatisfaction, weeping and cursing. Some simply stared at Mr. Burke's closed door with hostility. I went over to Tom and Jill. They looked as displeased as everyone else but were not vocal about it.

"Are you going to have enough money to get home, Sandy?" asked Jill with her forehead puckered in concern.

"No, I'm not. At least, I don't think so. Do you think Mr. Burke would loan me some money, if I ask him nicely. . .or beg?

"Not sure," said Tom, shaking his head sadly. "Maybe we can spot you what you need, if it's not too much."

"Thank you, but you need your money for your own needs!"

"Yeah, that's true, but we're probably in better shape than you are. We'll figure out something. Okay? But, Sandy," he said, lowering his voice a notch, "you're a lady of faith. Trust in God. I'm sure He wants you to get home as much as you do."

I nodded, tearing up as usual when someone was being nice to me, thanked Tom for his kind words, and headed for my sanctuary. I had to smile through my tears. I appreciated Tom's comment because I did trust in God, and I knew in my heart that He did want me to go home. In fact, I wouldn't be surprised if God was speaking directly to me through Tom. One way or another, I was becoming more confident that I would be able to go home.

I was aware now that coming down here to Cartagena was a terrible mistake, but that's all it was: a mistake. God may not have been *for* me coming here, but He did give us free will, so in a sense, He let me make my own decision. Nor did He send any signs, or warnings to stop me, which I interpreted now to mean that, despite all the difficulties I've been having, my adventure down here was going to end on a happy note. I was going to go home. Likewise, it was nobody's fault that I got sick, neither God's nor mine nor Carol's and Lori's for suggesting I come down here. It was just that my body couldn't seem to fight off the illnesses. I certainly did not believe they were inflicted upon me by Satan, as Job did. It was my own inability to fight illness that got me in this predicament.

No, the God I worship doesn't punish people for making mistakes. The God I worship and trust with my life is loving and kind, has compassion for the suffering of all His people and freely gives His strength and support to those who seek it. I had sought it over and over again and I had received His blessing numerous times. Even if I blamed God for the illnesses, the communists' attack in the *barrio*, or anything else that had occurred these past three months, I knew in my heart of hearts that God was greater and more powerful than my puny anger. His love could overwhelm it ten times over.

God loves me completely, just as I am. We are all His precious children made in His image. He has compassion for everybody. All we need to do is to stay faithful to Him, pray often, read His Word and praise His Holy Name. He will be faithful to His covenant with us and keep His promises to us.

Oh God, I prayed now, *give me courage and confidence to go and confront Mr. Burke one more time, to ask him for an advance or a loan, so I can pay for my ticket home. As You righted the wrongs done to Job, please, Lord, right this wrong, too. Help me to confront Mr. Burke. Help me get back home.*

I started to feel better right away. His peace gently settled on me and I felt Him fill me with the courage and confidence I had asked for to deal with Mr. Burke. As I headed for Mr. Burke's office now, I also felt sure that God had planted the idea in my mind to go and talk to Mr. Burke one more time. If that was true, then God would bless the outcome! Gathering myself up to my full height (such as it was) and taking a deep breath, I knocked on his door. I heard him call "Enter," so I did. He looked up at me warily, but didn't say anything. His look was cold, stern, almost challenging. He knew what I came to ask him. I had no doubt about that!

"Mr. Burke," I began, my voice nice and firm, "I need to ask you a favor."

"I know," he interrupted sharply. "You need more money! I heard you the first time! Everyone needs more money! Everyone's got a crisis and they've been in here to beg for an advance! I suppose that's what you want too!" He was scowling, annoyed at me and the whole situation. I tried to think kindly of him: you're rich, you don't know how hard it is for people like us. Or, thinking less kindly, maybe you don't want to know and that's why you live in a home near the Caribbean, far removed from us. I told myself to breathe and tried again.

"Sir, I have to get back to the States! My plane leaves next week, on Tuesday, and I don't have enough money to pay for my ticket!"

He studied me in silence for a long minute. "It's not my policy to give advances," he said less sharply. "You'll have to wait until the next paycheck."

I know my mouth dropped open and my eyes widened. Was he really going to say *no??*

"But I need the rest of the last two paychecks to pay for the ticket!" I said urgently. I was beginning to feel desperate. But Mr. Burke simply shook his head no.

I was so sure that he was going to help me out. *God*, I prayed, *soften his heart, please soften his heart!*

"Mr. Burke," I began again, feeling the shakiness in my voice, now, "The doctor was adamant about me leaving as soon as possible and next Tuesday's flight is the first one I could get! Please! Help me!" My desperation was very close to the surface, I could tell. I was ready to get down on my knees and beg. I was already crying.

He was silent for so long I thought I'd burst from holding my breath waiting for an answer.

Then he said the magic words I had prayed to hear: "How much do you need?" Without waiting for my reply, he pulled out his wallet and counted out some bills. "Here's fifty dollars," he said gruffly. "That's all I can spare." He held the money out to me and I had to walk humbly over to him to get it. God had moved this man's hard heart to help me! *Thank you, Lord God Almighty! Thank you for touching Mr. Burke's heart!*

"Thank you so much, Mr. Burke! Thank you!" I blubbered. He nodded briefly, then dismissed me.

"Oh," he said when I was at the door, "don't tell the others. They'll all come back in and want a handout too!" I barely heard him but nodded automatically and closed the door behind me. The word "handout" stung. He had to say that! He was already back to his old self. Suddenly, I noticed everyone's eyes were fastened on me as I stood at his closed door. I sensed their two silent questions: Did he help you out? Would he help me, too?

Rosita motioned me over. "Tell me," she whispered. The others closed in around us, wanting to hear my answer. What should I do? Keep quiet because Mr. Burke told me to? Or tell them, probably engendering more discontent since they'd already asked for help and were refused. What a dilemma! I decided to just shake my head, as if overwhelmed, which was the truth.

"I have to go," I told Rosita softly and retreated to the library where I could close the door and praise God for softening Mr. Burke's heart enough to help me and pray he would help the others, too.

A short time later, Mr. Burke came thundering out of his office. "Where is everybody?" he demanded. I could hear him loud and clear through the library door. Rising, I went out to be with the others as they stared at him in bewilderment. "Where are all the students?" he bellowed. Everybody froze like deer blinded by a car's headlights. "Well? Somebody say something!" he demanded.

Tom stepped forward slowly. "Sir, we cancelled the classes."

"What?! Why?"

Tom, though nervous, kept his eyes steadily on Mr. Burke's and explained," We were all upset because you hadn't come in with our paychecks, so we decided to cancel the classes and drive out to your home to get the checks. That was when you arrived. Sir." Mr. Burke glared at Tom and Tom just stared right back. The tension in the lobby was palpable. More quietly, Tom went on, "Sir, several of the staff are really desperate for their full paychecks. They have crises and great need in their families."

Mr. Burke thundered, "I can't produce what I don't have!" Tom's look challenged him but he refrained from saying anything. Mr. Burke scowled and stared at everyone. There was a long silence.

Rosita stepped forward slowly. "Sir," she said quietly, "Leona's mother will die in a matter of days without her medication; she is extremely sick. Leona doesn't have enough money to get the medicine. Whatever you can spare, sir, even if only a few *pesos*, could you please help her out?"

"But then you'll all want something," he growled back at her.

"No, sir. No one else will ask you for money." She immediately turned and look uncertainly at the others since she hadn't cleared this with them first. As if it had all been prearranged, however, each one nodded his or her agreement. Rosita, a flicker of pride and gratitude passing over her face, turned back to Mr. Burke. "We will all wait until the next paycheck," she assured him, "but Leona, she really, really needs help right now or her mother will die. Please, Mr. Burke, will you help?" I glanced surreptitiously at Leona. She was aware of what Rosita was saying, but she kept her head down sobbing silently.

Mr. Burke looked from one person to another. Each one nodded his or her agreement with what Rosita had promised. Finally, he turned his gaze on Leona. Then, with a sigh, he reached for his wallet and pulled out a couple of bills, handed them to Rosita to give to Leona and returned stiffly to his office, closing the door firmly behind him. Rosita hurried back to her friend and pushed the money into her hand, closing her fingers over it. Leona looked up at her, eyes bright with tears.

"Vaya!" urged Rosita. Go! *"Ahorita!"* Leona looked at the others, who all nodded their encouragement. Aurelio even took her hand and led her to the top of the stairs. She looked around at everyone, still hesitant, her awareness of their sacrifice showing on her face.

"Vaya!" we all chorused. She took a deep breath, pulled out a hanky to wipe her tears away, and ran down the stairs.

.   .   .

Over the weekend, I sorted out the last of my clothes. I kept enough to get me home on Tuesday, and put all the rest (not that there were many clothes left, mind you) on display for Carmen when she came Sunday evening. I also planned to sell her all of Joe's things that I'd brought from his apartment and the set of silverware and dishes I'd bought for my guests. I would keep my satchel to put in whatever stuff I had left to take home and sell my two suitcases to Carmen since I wouldn't need them anymore (both were years old and looked the worse for wear).

Carmen bought everything I'd laid out for her! True, she never refused anything I'd offered her, but I was super pleased she bought everything this time. She went to the window and motioned her son, who was parked outside, to come and help carry the things to their car (I'd seen him several times when he delivered and picked her up each time she came by my apartment). I waved goodbye to the two of them, then returned to the apartment to count out how many *pesos* I'd made. I had earned the most *pesos* ever! Hopefully, when all my monies were put together, I would have enough money at last to pay for my ticket home.

When I went to the bank on Monday morning, all the *pesos* from Carmen converted into seventy-five American dollars. Would that be enough, I wondered, along with the fifty dollars Mr. Burke gave me and the left-over American Express checks I'd brought from home? It was going to be very, very close! However, I reminded myself, God knew what my situation was and I felt Him assuring me that He would make it enough to get me home. So, with a sigh of confidence, I relaxed and smiled and walked on to the school. Just in case all the money I'd collected wasn't enough, I knew I would be prepared to work at the school for another two weeks and try again then. Either way, I was no longer afraid because I fully believed that God would keep me healthy (or stubborn) enough to wait two more weeks if I had to. Of course, I prayed that I'd going home tomorrow.

. . .

Arriving at the school, I put some finishing touches on the library and checked that books were in order on the shelves and ready to be checked out. The library was starting to get more business lately, also, from the staff, the teachers and even the students. I had devised a card file system for readers and for checked-out books that was working well.

Julio and Aurelio came in to see me.

"What's up?" I asked.

"Do you need a ride to the airport tomorrow morning?" asked Julio.

My mouth dropped open. In all the excitement of collecting my money together, I'd completely forgotten about transportation to the airport!

"As a matter of fact, I do," I answered them.

"We will take you."

"That would be wonderful!" I hugged each of them. "Thank you both so much!" I was so grateful because I didn't think I'd have enough money to pay for a taxi and the ticket, too. They also told me they would make arrangements for the apartment furniture to be picked up and that they and Rosita would clean the apartment afterwards. What wonderful, wonderful people they were! *God bless them!*

I took time to say goodbye to Rosita and Leona before my classes began. I would really miss them. Rosita, in particular, had been such a good friend. Her boyfriend, she whispered excitedly to me, was getting ready to propose to her so I knew her future was set. Leona looked more relaxed now that her mother was doing better and gave me a beautiful homemade thank you card. I hugged both of them for a long time. "Thank you!" Leona whispered in my ear and kissed me on the cheek.

The Hindes joined us. Jill said, "We wish you the best of luck, Sandy! We hope you get your health back quickly! Write to us," she urged. "I wrote our address down on this piece of paper. We really want to hear from you, to know how you're doing, and what you do with your life from tomorrow on."

"Okay, I will! Let me write my address and phone number down, too, because I want to hear how things go here at the school after I leave."

"Right," agreed Tom. "Absolutely." We hugged and patted each other on the back. I was going to miss them both. Tom had such a sense of justice about him. I was impressed with his willingness to stand up for the staff when Mr. Burke tried to take advantage of them. Jill? She was just so sweet and caring, as well as such a great teacher. They made a super couple.

To my surprise, Archie showed up then. "What's all the excitement about?" he asked.

"Well," said Tom, "got an hour?"

Archie's eyebrows raised up and he peered over his glasses, which, as usual, had slipped down on his nose. "I've got as long as it takes, I guess."

"Okay," said Tom, "let's go find a seat some place where we can talk privately." We headed back to Daisy's, selected a table and sat.

"To begin with," said Tom, "we had a big run-in with Mr. Burke over docked paychecks. Are you aware of this?"

"I know I only got half a paycheck last time. I haven't gotten the current paycheck yet. That's why I came in today."

"Well, this time it's not much more. Sandy had to beg Burke for more money so she could pay for her ticket home. We all confronted Burke on Leona's behalf to get some extra money for her mother's medicine. It was not a pleasant scene, but I think he knew there was going to be mutiny if he didn't cough up some dough for these two women."

Archie shook his head, then looked at me and told me he was glad I got the money I needed to go home. "Well," he then commented in his soft voice, "I guess I better go get my pay, if Burke is here."

"He is," we told him.

When Archie stood, he paused and turned to me, "When do you leave, Sandy?"

"Tomorrow morning."

"Then I'd like to take a moment to say goodbye to you now, because this is the last time I'll see you." Tom and Jill got the hint and left. I stood up. "I want you to know something, Sandy." He took my hands in his and looked me straight in the eye. "I have found you one of the most charming young women I've ever met, sick or not. You are desirable, you are beautiful in looks and spirit, you have compassion for people, and you're an excellent teacher. I've already told you I love you. I still do. I want you to get well, okay?"

"I'm going to do my best."

"Sandy, I'll remember you the rest of my life."

My heart pounded so loudly I thought sure he could hear it. He really was such a sweet guy, and if this adventure did have the possibility of romance in it, it would most likely be with Archie. . .except for the nude photos he wanted to take. That part turned me off. He draw me close to him until our chests touched and planted a tender kiss on my lips. He put his hands through my hair and pulled my face closer to him, his tongue entering my mouth and starting to play with my tongue.

I pulled away from him. "No, Archie," I murmured.

"Why? We're alone. I want to love you."

"No, it's too late. I'm leaving tomorrow, remember?" He let me go.

"I wanted something to remember you by," he said plaintively.

"I'm sorry, Archie. I can't. I'm ready to go home, emotionally. I've already said goodbye to everyone else. I just want to go home and get better."

He stood there a long moment, absorbing what I said. "So this is goodbye, then?"

"Yes."

Archie didn't ask for my address or phone number, nor did he make any promises to get in touch with me. We stood there like two bumps on a log staring at each other. I feared I had hurt his feelings badly.

"Archie, I want to thank you – " I started, but he put his finger on my lips to quiet me. Then he slipped a hand into his pocket and pulled out a picture. It was of the two of us, arms around each other's waist, smiling at the person taking the picture.

"Keep it," said Archie. "Remember me. I'll always remember you." With a quick final kiss, he turned and walked away. I stood there for a long time, wondering if I had made a terrible mistake brushing Archie off too hastily. Could I have fallen in love with him if we had more time together? I searched my heart. No, I concluded, Archie was not the one I would marry. I was not unaware of what my family would think of me marrying a black man.

Please, Lord, I pray that You will help Archie find someone to love and to be loved by in return. Help him understand how anxious I am to go home; how unable I am to invest in a deep emotion like love right now. I pray also for Aurelio, that You might heal his eyes and let him continue to see and that Julio might find happiness with his wife and children.

Please Lord, also be with Rosita and Leona. May they find happiness.
And bless Tom and Jill for their kind-heartedness.

     .   .   .

I taught my last two classes that evening. The students were all curious about why classes had been cancelled on Friday and wanted to know if there was a problem and would it happen again. I could tell they were a bit indignant that we had done such a thing. The Hindes and I had decided to tell them there had been an emergency, but the problem was now solved and classes wouldn't be canceled any more. Naturally, they wanted to know what the emergency had been, but I only smiled at them and shook my head.

I also informed them that tonight was my last night to teach them, that I was leaving Cartagena in the morning to return to the United States.

"No, Miss! Why, Miss?"

"Personal reasons," I answered.

"Did we do something wrong?"

"No! No, no one did anything wrong! The reason is that I need to go home to be with my family."

They looked sad and just sat quietly, taking it in. I felt bad, like I was letting them down. First Archie, now these wonderful, eager students.

I had them work in their workbooks for the rest of the class and when I dismissed them I received hugs and words of encouragement from each one of them as they filed out the door.

This was the end of my adventure in Cartagena, Colombia.

     .   .   .

Tuesday, September 3, 1963: My last day.

Julio and Aurelio arrived at the apartment bright and early and collected my meager belongings to carry down to the truck. Once stashed in the bed of the truck, we took off for the airport. All three of us were quiet; nobody seemed to have much to say.

"Are you guys alright?" I asked as we neared the airport parking lot.

"No," said Julio bluntly. "I'm going to miss you.

"Me, too," said Aurelio.

Julio parked the car and Aurelio picked up my satchel, but they didn't start walking into the airport right away. I looked at the two of them, wondering why.

"I really like you, Sandy," said Julio, hugging me. "I don't want you to go – but I know you're sick and you have to. I'll miss you more than I can tell you."

"I'll miss you too, Julio, and you too, Aurelio." I took each of their hands in mine and gazed earnestly at them. "I want you to know that I am so very, very glad I've met you two. You've been caring and protective and helpful the whole time I've been here.. I wish you two were my brothers! I always feel safe when I'm with you." Both of them embraced me and kissed my cheeks.

"You thin," commented Aurelio, holding me at arm's length to inspect me. "Not good," he pronounced solemnly.

"My Mom will fatten me up when I get home," I told him, laughing. "She's a great Italian cook!"

"Italian? You Italian, like me?"

"Yes, I am!"

"Good! Eat spaghetti! Have your Italian mother cook spaghetti for you, every day, fatten you up!"

We were all laughing now, the tension broken. They went with me through customs and out to the tarmac and then walked me over to the stairs going up into the plane. For a moment it looked like they were going to climb up the stairs with me! Instead, they paused at the bottom and gave me one last heart-felt hug and kiss, then turned and left.

I have to admit I boarded the plane with mixed emotions. Everyone at the school had been so good to me, although Mr. Burke's behavior was questionable. Yet, he did give me $50.00, and his wife, Helen, was definitely nice. As for his pocketing that money from the safe, seen by Joe Bastien, it remained an unsolved mystery at this point. I was going to miss everyone else dearly. We had cared for each other, supported each other, laughed with each other, even cried with each other. I knew I would never forget them.

Moments later, the plane began to taxi away from the airport and I was officially on my way home.

When we finally arrived in the United States, I had a layover in Miami before continuing to Buffalo. As I milled around with the other people, seeing lots of food in the various cafes, I realized I was actually hungry. I hadn't eaten since lunch the day before and I yearned for one of Daisy's special donuts and a cup of coffee. The problem was, I only had *one dime* left to my name after paying for my ticket, and that wasn't enough for anything. You see, God did make sure I was able to pay for my ticket home, but I sure didn't have much spending money left afterwards!

I was sorely tempted to ask someone for a couple of dollars so I could get something to eat. I looked around at the folks: family groups, singles, couples, threesomes. My eyes lighted on an American family of father, mother, and three small children. I accidently caught the mother's eye and swiftly turned away. I wasn't going to – I wouldn't – beg. *But please, God, I'm hungry!* I could almost hear God reminding me that His Son had known hunger, too, for forty days in the wilderness, and the devil had tempted Him to ask God to send angels down to feed him. I don't know if the devil was tempting me right now, but I did ask God to send an angel to help me.

A moment later, I felt someone tapping me on the shoulder. I turned around and looked up at the mother from the American family standing beside me, smiling down at me.

"Hello," she said. "I was wondering if you'd like to join us. There's plenty of room at our table. You look so lonely." *Was she the angel of God I'd just prayed for?* I didn't know what to say. How could I sit at their table and watch them eat in front of me? I was in a quandary and my palms started to sweat and my heart to beat fast.

"Please," she coaxed. She offered me her hand and, barely aware of what I was doing, I let myself take it and be led over to her table. I joined them and sat down, but I couldn't look at anyone or the food on the table. The children took no real notice of me, for which I was glad. They must be used to their parents picking up strays, I thought. Instead of being curious about me, they went right on eating and chattering with each other.

"Are you alright?" asked the father. I turned toward him briefly and nodded, then lowered my head again. His eyes were so probing. The mother slowly reached over and lifted my chin up.

"What's wrong?" she asked, concerned. I couldn't answer her.

"Are you hungry?" asked the father. Was it that obvious? I closed my eyes and started to cry. I really was an emotional and physical wreck! The mother wanted to hurry over to the counter and order a big breakfast for me, like eggs, bacon and pancakes. I told her I couldn't eat all that, that I'd be happy with a cup of coffee and maybe a donut or sweet roll.

Then I blurted out, "But, I can't pay for it! I only have a dime left!"

"Shh," soothed the mother. "It's okay. I'll be right back."

"I don't know if this will help you," said the father quietly after she left, "but I'm an ordained minister of God. My name is Reverend Dick Mason, my wife's name is Sally. In my line of work, feeding the hungry is one of our greatest privileges. Our church runs a food kitchen for the homeless, and it gives me great pleasure to help people in whatever situation they find themselves. So, don't worry about the cost of your breakfast. I think we can cover it! God loves you, and He wants you to be filled!"

I was awestruck! This family *was* sent to me by God!

I tried not to wolf down the English muffin that the mother had gotten me. I tried to eat it slowly. The coffee, however, was just the right temperature and slid right down. When I'd eaten everything, boy, did I feel better! It looked like I was getting my appetite back!

The children began to slide down in their seats and doze off. The Masons and I sat and talked about their ministry and about my experiences in Cartagena until it was time for me to catch my next flight. I thanked these kind people over and over for their generosity and kindness to me. I truly believe that God put them in my path to feed me physically and spiritually. We hugged all around and I left for the rest of my flight home.

The last leg of my flight was more relaxing, now that I'd eaten. I dozed for a couple of hours. When I awoke, I passed the time leafing through a magazine in the pocket of the seat in front of me. The closer I got to Buffalo, however, the more my excitement grew. I was almost home! Then I thought about having to see a doctor and prayed he would be able to cure me. The thought did occur to me that the doctor at the University in Cartagena was urging me to go home so I would die there and not in Cartagena!

But now, this close to home, I no longer felt like I was dying. Not that I was feeling as well as I did in June before leaving for Colombia, mind you. More like I was feeling safer the closer I got to Buffalo and good medical help. At least, the medicine Dr. Chavez gave me was starting to work; I was starting to feel some better. Since my appetite was starting to come back, I felt hope blooming again that there would be a future for me, that I would be fully healed. I began to entertain thoughts about what to do with the rest of my life. I definitely wanted to spend a good long time with Nana, Mom and Don.

I made up my mind that once I was all better, I'd re-enroll in Lancaster Seminary and enter the ordained ministry, as I had initially planned. I was sure it was already too late to start this fall, but maybe I could start in January. I decided I'd call the seminary in the next day or so to make that arrangement. In the meantime, I could get a job in a library to earn some money to pay for seminary. It was a plan! Looking out the window, I began to see the steel mills in South Buffalo and my heart started racing in anticipation of seeing my family again. I glanced down at myself, at clothes that hung too loose on me, at how old and faded they looked. Did I look old and faded, too?

Deplaning at last at the Buffalo airport, I spied Nana, Mom, Don and Phil right away. They started waving and I waved back, a big grin on my face. When we got close enough, Mom's arms were outstretched, so I rushed into them, and let her envelop me and cuddle me as if I were her little girl again. I was bawling from relief and happiness, so glad to be home. Because I sent a letter to them last week about my health issues, they now held me at arm's length to look me over. No one said anything, but the looks they exchanged were telling enough: I looked sick; I'd lost weight; my hair was an uneven curly mess (I'd tried to cut it myself); my clothes had become shabby-looking.

They started heading for the luggage carousel, but I stopped them. "I just have my satchel here. No suitcases. We can just go to the car and leave." Their eyes were filled with questions.

"Let's wait until we get in the car, then Sandy can explain," said Don. So that's what we did. We were barely in the car driving out of the airport when they started hurling questions at me. Why only the satchel? Where were the two suitcases? What about your fever and the other illnesses? Tell us about the communists. Tell us about the school.

Too many questions were coming at me at once, so I stopped trying to answer any of them. Most of the questions came from Mom, with Don a close second, and Phil trailing. Nana sat quietly in the back with Phil and me trying to listen to everyone. When it quieted down, I asked if we could wait until we got home for me to explain everything. To my surprise, they agreed. For the next ten minutes or so, I looked out the window at familiar streets, restaurants, hotels, and stores. Then we were home.

In the house, Phil ran my suitcase up the stairs to my bedroom and then ran right back down, apparently not wanting to miss a word of what

I had to say. It felt good to be surrounded by all of my family. Mom took me by the shoulders and sat me down in a comfortable upholstered chair in the living room where we were all standing.

"Now," she said in her 'mother voice,' "you can tell us all about everything. Start at the beginning and tell us the whole story. I promise we won't interrupt you."

"Do you want to hear what the doctor told me first, or last?"

"Start with the doctor," they all agreed.

"Okay." So I told them all about it, leaving nothing out. My sunburn was mostly gone but I told them about that, too. They listened without interruption, as they promised (which was very rare for them, believe me). Then they sat there in silence while slowly digesting the news and shaking their heads in dismay.

Finally, Phil spoke up. "What exactly is 'paratyphoid fever'?" I explained that it was a form of typhoid fever and involved a high fever that was hard to bring down. I told them that my fever was 40.3 in Celsius, but I didn't know what that was in Fahrenheit.

"Let me get the medical dictionary from Britannica (Encyclopedia) and look it up," said Don. He went out to his car to retrieve it.

While Don was gone, Phil asked, "What's 'amoebic dysentery'?"

"Think uncontrollable diarrhea," I told him. He made a disgusted face just at the thought of it.

Don returned with the medical dictionary and concentrated on finding the Celsius-Fahrenheit conversion table. When he did, I could see him running his finger down the column, looking for 40.3. His finger stopped moving and he looked up at me sharply.

"What does it equal?" I asked, not sure I really wanted to know any more because of the look on his face.

"40.3 Celsius equals *104.5 degrees Fahrenheit*! My God!" There was a collective gasp from everyone in the room. That was one high fever! No one spoke for a moment. I knew my temperature had been high because of the reaction of the doctor who had taken it and Rosita's big eyes when she touched my forehead. I could tell my family was just as shocked.

"So, what you had was a 104.5 degree temperature, plus the rest of the infections, all at the same time," summarized Don. I nodded. Mom came over, stood me up and hugged me long and hard. "I'm so sorry we let you go down there," she murmured in my ear. The others came over and embraced me, too. It felt so good, exactly what I'd needed after the past three long months!

"Okay," said Mom, standing back. "I think that's about all we can handle tonight." Then she shifted gears and changed the subject. "Did you eat on the plane? Are you hungry?"

"No, and I am a little hungry. I think I would like to have a glass of milk and a piece of toast, or something like that."

"How about a grilled cheese sandwich?"

"Perfect!"

"Coming right up," said Mom brightly. She and Nana went out to the kitchen to get things ready.

Don came over to me and studied my eyes. "You don't look well, Sandra, and you've lost too much weight. You're skin and bones." I could only nod. My stepfather and I didn't always get along, so the concern he was showing me now was very touching.

"Mom will fatten me up again," I assured him.

"I know she will. Starting now. Go out and eat your sandwich." He started to scowl, but I knew he wasn't angry, just very concerned about me." I joined Mom and Nana in the kitchen. Though they had a big table in the dining room, I preferred to eat in their little kitchen nook. Phil came in and joined us. The grilled cheese sandwich melted in my mouth and went down oh so easily. Not having had real milk for three months, I thoroughly enjoyed it now and savored it.

It was only about 8:00 pm, but I felt weary from holding in all the anxiety of the past three months and dealing with my illnesses. There was also the excitement of coming back home. My eyelids started to droop.

"Tomorrow," said Mom, "I'm taking you to my doctor to get a full examination.

"Okay," I nodded, yawning.

"I think our girl is ready for bed," commented Nana.

"I am," I agreed, rising from my chair. Mom went upstairs with me. She got a quizzical look on her face when she saw my lonely satchel sitting there. "Okay, where are your suitcases?" she asked. "I didn't hear your answer in the car."

"Well, I had to sell almost everything I had to pay for my ticket home. What I had left fit in the satchel, so I sold the two suitcases."

"What do you mean you had to sell everything? I thought they were supposed to pay your way *back* from Cartagena, like they paid your way *to* Cartagena."

I looked at Mom in surprise. The flyer I read back in May did say transportation would be paid both ways! "I'll have to look into that," I said. "The Director of the school didn't seem to be aware of it. As for having to sell everything, I'll tell you all about it tomorrow." Mom took the satchel off the bed and pulled down the sheet and blanket for me. Then she hugged me tightly and kissed me goodnight without saying another word. I think she was fighting tears.

Wednesday morning, I got a look at myself in a full-length mirror. Skinny! I hadn't looked this thin since the beginning of high school! Next, I cautiously got on the scale – *95 lbs.! I'd lost 25 lbs. in less than three months' time!*

Mom knocked at the bedroom door. "Come in!" I called. She saw me in the bathroom, stepping off the scale.

"What did it say?" she asked, so I told her; her eyes filled with concern. "My poor baby! What did you weigh before you went down there?"

"Around 120."

"I'll put in a call to the doctor as soon as his office opens! I want him to do a complete physical on you and get you better! I'll put the weight back on you, if I have to feed you spaghetti every day!" I chuckled. Since Mom, Nana and I were all Italian, spaghetti was a big deal in our family, but Don (an Irishman) was a great cook, too, so I had no doubt they'd all take turns at fattening me up. But I did hope it wouldn't all be spaghetti, since that was what I had subsisted on in Cartagena for almost three months!

. . .

At the doctor's later that day, he indeed did give me a full examination from head to toe and took many vials of blood and a urine sample. He also asked for all my symptoms of the various illnesses I had, and I handed him the information sheet given me by Dr. Chavez. Sitting in his office afterward with Mom, waiting to get his report, I was fidgety. What if he confirmed everything the doctor in Cartagena said I had? What if I was still sick enough to die?

The doctor entered the office briskly and sat at his desk. He wasn't a very tall man, but he had a commanding presence. "Ms. Cone," he began, and I sat up straighter, my heart beating fast with nervousness.

"You are a very sick young woman!" he said, looking me straight in the eyes. "You have everything the Colombian doctor said you had. Consider yourself 'Typhoid Mary' for the next year! (*Typhoid Mary?*) You must wash your hands thoroughly whenever you handle food, especially if you cook for other people. I'm going to prescribe enough medicine to rid you of all the other infections, but you must do your part by taking your medications faithfully, eating healthy and exercising. The paratyphoid fever will take a few more weeks, possibly months to resolve. You'll continue to feel feverish and listless, or even cold and shivery, but it will eventually pass. Be patient, okay?" (There's that word again!)

"Yes sir," I said meekly. Unspoken but clear was the new and improved message: *I was going to get better! I was going to live! Thank you, thank you, Lord!*

When Mom and I got home, I called the seminary and actually spoke with the director himself, Dr. Robert Moss. I explained that I had contacted the seminary back in May about putting off my arrival there for another year since I had accepted a teaching fellowship in Colombia. However, I was back from Colombia early and would like to start in the second semester, if that were possible. I took a breath and held it, waiting for his reply.

"You know," he said, "we are just starting our fall session right now. People are arriving and getting settled as we speak. On Monday we will actually begin with an all school retreat. If you could get here by Monday morning, you could actually begin this semester."

"But I'm broke," I told him, my voice catching. "I used up all my money just to get home from Colombia."

"Not to worry. I'll help you take out a student loan to cover your expenses here. We'll make it work!" Stunned by his remarks, I barely knew what to say, but "Okay!" slipped out of my mouth unbidden.

"Excellent!" he responded. "Will you be driving or flying? We can meet you at the airport if you want." I told him I'd have to let him know after I talked with my parents.

I hung up, awed by this unexpected turn of events. Wow! I wasn't going to have to put my life on hold. I could keep on marching forward right now. Smiling happily, I hurried down to tell my parents about this new development, expecting them to be as joyful as I was. Unfortunately, they definitely weren't – especially Don.

"How are you going to pay for it?" he demanded, his eyes boring into mine. My happiness shifted to uncertainty at his brusque manner. I told him about the student loan the seminary president would help me get. Don scowled and shook his head, not at all happy with the idea. With lips pursed, he turned away from me. I looked toward Mom for some support, but she wouldn't look at me. Her eyes were downcast and her shoulders slumped. I didn't know what to say or do next.

Don turned back to me and angrily asked, "What about your health problems? What about spending some time with your mother? What about working to earn money to go to seminary? What about being able to buy new clothes that fit you before you go?"

I had no answer for him. His questions were all valid. On the other hand, Mom and Don hadn't made much time for me while I was growing up. They hadn't helped to pay for my college education. They lived all around the country, wherever Don was assigned a territory to sell Britannica Encyclopedias and I barely saw them once a year. As for my health problems, I could heal at seminary just as easily as I could at home. And as for money, I'd have the loan to pay for seminary, food and lodging, and I could work part-time to earn money for books, clothes and other incidents.

The stumbling block was getting to seminary. With Don's attitude, I couldn't ask him to drive me or pay for a bus ticket, and flying was totally out of the question. I sighed and sat down at the kitchen table, just as forlorn as Mom was. A long, awkward silence ensued. I finally just got up and left, not sure what else to do. I could talk with Nana, but even if she loaned me the money for bus fare, she'd also have to pay for a taxi to get me to the bus station since she didn't drive and had no car.

I retreated to my room, got on my knees, and prayed. *Father, only You know the solution to this problem. If it is Your will that I go to seminary this fall, please make a way possible for me to get there. I'm sorry to always be troubling You with problems. Please forgive me.*

Laying on my bed, I closed my eyes and let go of my anxiety, putting it in God's capable hands. I slept for a while.

Later on, I went back downstairs, not sure what exactly to expect. Everyone was sitting in the living room and Don motioned me over. I sat down and waited for him to say what he had to say.

"We've been discussing this," he said, "and we understand you really want to go to Lancaster this fall. But I'm concerned about paying off that loan. Britannica sales aren't so good right now, which means we're not in a position to pay it off."

"You don't have to," I interjected. "The loan won't be due until after I graduate and have a job, at which point I'll be in a position to pay the loan off myself."

Don was surprised. "I don't understand."

"Student loans are set up so they don't come due for payment until you're in a position to pay."

"And you'll pay it off, not us?"

"Yes."

He looked at Mom and Nana, then back to me. "Okay," he said doubtfully. "The next questions is, how do you plan to get to Lancaster?"

"I don't know."

Mom spoke up then. "Do you really want to go to Lancaster right now, not later in the year or next year?"

"I'd like to, yes."

She and Don exchanged glances. "Okay, then," said Don, resigned, "we'll drive you to the school."

"Thank you," I whispered, but I didn't feel very relieved. Mom was sad-looking, Don was subdued, and Nana just sat quietly with her hands folded in her lap.

"I'm concerned about your health," commented Mom then.

"I'm going to get better," I assured her.

"And you need new clothes before you go. We'd need to go shopping right away." I could only nod, not trusting my voice because, even despite the thought of getting new clothes, the sadness lingering in the room was overpowering. It was like they were taking my desire to go to Lancaster as a personal affront, a rejection of them.

"Nana? What do you think about this?" I asked.

She was hesitant to answer, but then said, "I know you've felt God calling you to go into the ministry for a long time. Perhaps God is opening this door for you to go to seminary now because you returned safely back from Colombia. If you feel well enough to go to class and study, then I think you should go."

"Thank you," I whispered, tearing up.

"Back to the loan," said Don. "That pays for your tuition and books and such, right?"

"Yes."

"What about other needs, like eating and incidentals?"

"I'll find a part-time job," I answered, hopefully one in the seminary library.

He shook his head, realizing he wasn't going to win this argument. "Okay," he said, "Your Mom wants us to drive you there, so that's what we'll do. We'll leave Sunday, spend the night in a motel, and arrive at Lancaster the next morning."

Tears of relief, mixed with tears of sadness, rolled down my cheeks. The sadness came from feeling like I was letting them down and also regretting that I only had only a few days to visit with Mom and Nana before leaving. But I smiled and hugged them, then went off to call the seminary and tell them of my arrival plans.

I spent a lot of time over the next few days going over the rest of my "misadventures" in Cartagena with my family – the lost-and-found suitcase, the mosquito welcoming committee, the mice, the rats, the bat, the mating cockroaches, the dive bomber. They alternated between laughing and grimacing. I also told them about the travelers, the music, the barrios and the missionaries. The last thing I mentioned was the communist attack. Mom told me they'd heard about the communists blocking transportation into Bogotá on the news. When they had checked their atlas to see how close Bogotá was to Cartagena, they worried about my safety. I assured them the two cities were miles and miles apart. I didn't mention the Luggage Man's attack.

Mom and Nana took me shopping the next day to get some new clothes. By Sunday, I was ready to go. As we left the house that Sunday, Don was grumpy again and Mom down in the dumps. It was clear that they still weren't quite ready for me to leave so soon. But I was ready. I sat in the back seat and held Nana's hand. She gave it a squeeze, assuring me I was doing the right thing. On the way to the seminary, I prayed. *Please, Lord, let my seminary experience be a positive one. Help Mom and Don through their feelings of anger and sadness.*

I got to thinking about Cartagena again. It had definitely been a mistake to go to there. On the other hand, I'd met some great people and taught some terrific students (like Roberto). I'd put a flailing library back on its feet. And I'd had great adventures in most of the barrios and was able to meet two delightful missionaries. I realized, then, that apart from my health issues, my stay in Cartagena was everything I'd hoped it would be. *Thank You, God, for helping me once again to put things in proper perspective! And, please, if it is Your will, let me find someone to love at seminary.*

And God heard my prayer.

EPILOGUE

I met the love of my life on the very first day that I arrived at Lancaster, in the very first hour. Everyone was at the all-school retreat and the leader had divided the students into small groups. When we introduced ourselves, I learned his name was Ralph. He was a shorty like me with brown hair and light brown eyes, and he was also from Buffalo, New York! I liked him on the spot.

A day or two later, I was walking toward an empty table to eat my lunch in the 'refectory' [seminary dining hall] and spied Ralph sitting about halfway between me and where I was headed. Suddenly, I felt the presence of God surround me and I could 'hear' God telling me that I was going to marry Ralph and I could 'see' God pointing directly at him! My heart started racing but I kept moving forward, my eyes on Ralph the whole time. I saw him talking and laughing with classmates at his table and fell instantly in love with his laugh, the way his eyes crinkled, and the ease he had being with people. I wondered if God was going to tell *him* that he was going to marry *me*? *Help me trust You, Lord. I know if You want this union to happen, it will.*

About a month later, Ralph came down to the basement of the seminary library, where I was shelving books (my hope of getting a part-time job in the seminary library came true during my first week there!). Ralph stopped at an empty desk sitting at the bottom of the stairs and perched on it, watching me go about my work. I didn't notice him at first, but when I saw him, my heart went into overtime.

"Sandy," he said, "I think I'm falling in love with you."

Wow! Picture fireworks and explosions!

However, I have to tell you that this wasn't as sudden as it sounds. We'd already been studying together, eating together, holding long theological discussions together – plus many personal ones – and discovered we had several mutual friends in Buffalo. We knew we both were developing feelings for each other; we just didn't know how to start talking about them. But now we would! Despite a dry mouth and my heart doing flip-flops, I squeaked out, "You are?"

He took a step toward me and I promptly dropped the library books I held and rushed to him. We embraced and I knew God had spoken to him. My heart bloomed with love.

A week later, I unexpectedly received a letter from Tom and Jill Hindes, my friends from the Cartagena American Language School. I read:

Hi Sandy!

Thought you'd like to know about the demise of our American-sponsored language schools in Colombia. All seven schools were closed down by the government agency in charge and Burke was arrested for embezzlement! They've already got an indictment against him and it appears his wife has left him. Nobody got their last paycheck and we were all out of a job the day they came for Burke. By the way, Burke was supposed to give you and Joe money for your travel back home, but he kept it for himself. Fortunately, Jill and I had enough money saved up. Anyway, how are you doing now? Are you any better? Write or call.

Signed, Tom and Jill.

Thankfully, he included his address and phone number in Colorado. I would write them back later.

During the rest of 1963 and into 1964, I continued to heal. I gained my weight back (and then some). I became my old self again, my faith stronger and unwavering, honed and augmented by God's faithful provision of answered prayer. I thrived at seminary, pulling the various parts of my faith together as I'd hoped to; learning to appreciate the Old Testament, which had been Jesus' Bible His whole life; learning how the New Testament built on the Old Testament and augmented it; learning how the Early Church spread the Gospel, the "good news," to other parts of the world. All the pieces began to fall into place, a puzzle coming together. God, Deliverer of the captives in Egypt; God, Comforter of the sick and lost; God, Champion of the marginalized and forgotten. How magnificent is my God!

Meanwhile, on the home front, I'd occasionally cook dinner for Ralph in my apartment, while I was still "Typhoid Mary." Single men on campus lived in the dorm while women (there weren't many of us) and married couples lived in small apartments. I was very careful to wash my hands thoroughly before touching any food, as I'd been instructed. Thank goodness Ralph never got sick.

I had one final surprise – my hair started falling out in handfuls every time I showered! I suspected it was from the high fever I'd had. My doctor confirmed it. Ralph (despite my hair falling out!) proposed to me and we set a date to marry in June. However, I didn't want bald spots on my head on my wedding day! Surely God would heal my balding head, I thought. So I turned again to Matthew 7:7, and read the familiar words: *"Ask, and it will be given you; seek, and you will find; knock, and it will be opened to you."* I prayed to God to stop my hair from falling out and within a month, it stopped! My curls were confused about which way to curl, but at least my hair was getting thicker again. (Was the hair falling out going to stop on its own? Probably. I choose to give God the glory for answering my prayer!). Now I was completely symptom-free, just in time for my wedding and the rest of the adventures – good ones and bad ones – in my life with my husband, friend and lover!

. . .

As I ponder all the events of this past year, I recognize that I had expected there to be high points and low ones, but there were so many surprises than I wasn't prepared for. Many were good surprises, like the staff at the school who became good friends and the "angels" – the Mason family in Miami – who nourished my body and my soul. I don't know how I would have made it home safely after those three difficult months without the support, caring and generosity of spirit of my Cartagenian friends and the Masons.

Other surprises were less enjoyable, of course, like the fever, the communists, the sunburn and the almost-rape. And the smaller unpleasant surprises of mosquito bites, brazen mice, a very scary bat and the giant rats.

But I learned a lot. I learned that God watched over me and never left my side. He Himself came to me in so many different ways: a breath of cool air; a calming sense of peace; Bible stories like the Book of Job; the healings of Jesus throughout the New Testament; and in many other ways I wasn't always aware of. Though I had moments of doubt when my physical conditions threatened to overwhelm me, God found a way to let me know He hadn't left my side. He was carrying me during those times.

Ultimately, my stint in Colombia turned out to be a blessing. I learned to turn to the Word of God to find support, release from worry and a reminder that God was still in control. At no time did God desert me. Praise be to the Father, Son and Holy Spirit!

Thank You, Healing God! You have been so faithful and gracious to me all my life. You have come to me so many times to still my fearful, anxious heart. Thank You for healing me of all my infirmities, Lord Jesus! Thank You for helping me see how close You were to me through all the pain and agony in Cartagena. Thank You, too, for all the good times and for remaining faithful to me, even when I faltered. I am eternally thankful! Amen and Amen!

Made in the
USA
Columbia, SC